D1028054
Sports New York

SPORTS NEW YORK

Where to Play, Learn, and Watch In and Around the Big Apple

STEVE SCHWARTZ

City & Company • New York

For Sarah Jane and Elisabeth

Library of Congress Cataloging-in-Publication Data
Schwartz, Steven, 1942-
Sports new york: where to play, learn, and watch/
by Steve Schwartz.
p. cm.
Includes index.
ISBN 1-885492-55-3
1. Sports—New York (State)—New York. 2. Sports facilities—New York (State)—New York—Directories. 3. Recreation centers—New York (State)—New York—Directories.
4. Parks—New York (State)—New York—Directories. I. Title.
GV584.5.N4S35 1998
796'.025'7471—dc21
98—5612 CIP

First Edition
Printed in the United States of America
City & Company 22 West 23rd Street, New York, NY 10010

Publisher's Note: Neither City & Company nor the author has any interest, financial or personal, in the locations listed in this book. No fees were paid or services rendered in exchange for inclusion in these pages. While every effort was made to ensure accuracy at the time of publication, please call ahead to confirm location and other details.

TABLE OF

CONTENTS

INTRODUCTION

New York, New York (It's a Helluva Town)

Sports is the only entertainment where, no matter how many times you go back, you never know the ending. —NEIL SIMON, playwright

WHAT IF YOU SAW A FULL-PAGE AD IN THIS SUNDAY'S PAPER ABOUT A NEW, ALL-INCLUSIVE SPORTS RESORT? It's a place where you can play baseball, football, basketball, paintball, volleyball, paddleball, stickball, netball, and racquetball. There are lakes to boat on, and rivers to fish in. There's hurling and there's curling. There are soccer and lacrosse fields, cricket and rugby pitches, ice and roller rinks, handball and tennis courts, and bike paths, running paths, and bridle paths. And not only that, but you can roll boccie balls and bowling balls, throw darts and Frisbees, and run alongside some people—or into others.

Want to shoot arrows? Certainly. Shoot pool? Absolutely. Play table tennis? Positively. Arm wrestle? OK. Climb rocks? Yes. Golf? Tee 'em up. Box? Put 'em up. Go skiing? Why not? Play squash? No problem. Badminton? Just wear your whites. Fence? En garde. Jump out of airplanes? Go for it. Swim? Splash away. Surf the net? Sure. Surf the ocean? Sure, dude.

Quite a place, huh? And there's more: It's a four-season resort where most of the activities are within easy traveling distance, and lots of them are *absolutely free.* Interested? Well, the resort is called New York, and you don't have to book a flight because you're already here.

This is the greatest city in the world for a long list of reasons, and somewhere near the top is the fact that you can play almost any sport you want here—indoors or outdoors, and summer, fall, winter, and spring. If you're interested in facilities, there are 627 baseball and softball fields in the five boroughs, plus 74 boccie, 33 cricket, and 18 football and soccer fields. You'll find 542 tennis courts, 43 swimming pools, 14 miles of beaches, 13 golf courses, and six ice rinks—plus more basketball, paddleball, handball, and volleyball courts than you can shake a stick at.

About nine million of us live and play in this town, and so *Sports New York* is for everyone. It contains just about anything you'd want to know about sports in the Big Apple: where to play them, where to learn them, and where to just hang out and watch other people play.

What's the Scope of the Book?

Although much of my research centered on Manhattan, I spent quite a bit of time in the other boroughs as well. I even went out-of-town because no matter how hard I looked, I just couldn't find a jai alai *fronton* easily accessible by subway. Also, there's not enough room in Tompkins Square Park for polo, not enough rapids in the Central Park reservoir for whitewater rafting, and if you tried to skydive in midtown, getting impaled on the spire of the Chrysler Building would be a real possibility. When necessary, there are out-of-town listings, but since I'm a real New Yorker, I did my best to discover facilities no more than an hour or so away from Times Square and accessible by public transportation.

Why Listen to Schwartz?

Ever hear the expression "You gotta sacrifice your body for love of the game"? Well here's my resume: broken fingers (baseball), bad knee (volleyball), pulled back muscles (whitewater rafting), broken nose (basketball), strained wrist (tennis), fractured arm (football), twisted ankle (racquetball), pulled hamstring (running), hyperextended elbow (squash)—and let's not forget the hook that embedded itself in my hand while I was learning to fish.

I've played or watched every sport mentioned in this book. In fact, I'm a "has been" or "used to be" in all the major ones, ready to stack up my credentials with the best of them. I've played football in the mud, basketball in the snow, and baseball in the rain. I've learned tennis in the scorching heat, volleyball in the dense fog, and Frisbee in the swirling wind. And I've watched boxing in the middle of a hurricane, and golf during a storm that featured hailstones larger than the golf balls.

How'd You Choose the Listings?

I wanted you, the sports fan, to know about what's going on and where, and to have as many choices as possible for locations where you can play, learn, and watch your favorite sport: uptown and downtown, East Side and West Side, in Manhattan and nearby. I included options with widely varying costs, so you'll find free ones (parks and schoolyards), inexpensive ones (rec centers and state parks), more expensive ones (Y's), and the most expensive ones (private clubs). Some of the facilities are listed because they provide the best and widest range of offerings, and others because they were one of the few places offering a particular sport.

Sports One-Stops

There are numerous city-run recreation centers and Y's scattered throughout the five boroughs, and they're *all* sports one-stops because of the wide array of programs offered. Besides Central Park, which is almost completely free (you do need a permit for some activities), the rec centers and Y's are the next least expensive choices for sports lovers. The rec centers are very inexpensive and the Y's, although their prices have risen a great deal over the years, still don't cost as much as the private clubs.

There are 22 YMCA's in the five boroughs, two YWCA's, and one YMHA, so there's likely to be one convenient to where you live or work. There's no single telephone number to call for information about all of them, so you'll have to try directory assistance or hit the phone book. As for the rec centers, you can call the following:

The Bronx: 718-430-1858
Brooklyn: 718-965-8940
Manhattan: 212-408-0204
Queens: 718-520-5936
Staten Island: 718-816-6172

The Big Five One-Stops

Central Park

Naturally, the greatest city in the world has the greatest park in the world. Resting on over 800 acres of land purchased in 1856 for 5.5 million dollars, Central Park is completely man-made. In an era when land was dug up by shovelfuls and removed by horsedrawn cart, it took 20,000 workers over 16 years to remove about ten million cartloads of debris, and replace it with enough earth and topsoil to plant more than 270,000 trees and shrubs.

As the city has changed, the park has as well. Originally designed for strolling and relaxing, its ball fields and tennis courts were added by the turn of the century, and eventually the roads were paved to accommodate automobiles. In the 1930's, the central reservoir was turned into the Great Lawn, the herd of 150 sheep in the Sheep Meadow were moved, and Tavern on the Green was built.

Today, you can play basketball here, as well as football, volleyball, croquet, tennis, baseball, softball, soccer, and Frisbee—not to mention run, bike, ride horseback, lawn bowl, fish, swim, climb rocks, ice skate, in-line and roller skate, racewalk, row, skateboard—and ride on an absolutely wonderful carousel.

Asphalt Green (212-369-8890)
555 East 90th Street at York Avenue

Asphalt Green is a terrific sports complex with an equally terrific success story. The facility sits on 5.5 acres that were once home to a municipal asphalt plant. When operations ceased, the city was flooded with proposals to build yet more high-rise apartments. But a group of neighborhood residents had a different idea and worked like the devil to make it happen. They collected petitions, convinced the city to reject the various apartment plans, and raised enough money to buy the land. The name Asphalt Green seemed particularly appropriate, and the current facility has an extraordinary swimming complex, playing fields, a gym, basketball courts, running track, and fitness center—as well as a theater and art studio. Asphalt Green is a nonprofit, self-supporting organization. Operating funds come from field and gym rentals, program revenues, pool and health club memberships, endowment income, and private contributions.

Riverbank State Park (212-694-3600)
Hudson River at 145th Street

A 23-acre facility built on a platform above the river, the park actually sits atop a sewage treatment plant, but it looks fabulous, with evergreens, lawns, trees, and flowers. Plus, there are walkways along the Hudson that provide some of the best river views in the city, complemented by the sight of the George Washington Bridge in the background.

After crossing the West Side Highway on a pedestrian bridge, you'll find buildings containing a 50-meter pool, a 200' x 85' covered skating rink (roller skating in the summer and ice skating in the winter), and a full size gym. Outside are two smaller pools, four basketball courts, four handball and paddleball courts, four tennis courts, and a four laps/mile, eight-lane track that circles an artificial turf football/soccer field. An inexpensive annual fee covers just about all the programs.

Reebok (212-362-6800) 160 Columbus Avenue between 67th and 68th Street

Without question this is the most completely equipped (and luxurious) sports club in town. It has six floors and 140,000 square feet of the following: a junior Olympic-size swimming pool, Jacuzzi, steam room, sauna, three basketball/volleyball courts, indoor soccer, six-laps/mile outdoor running track, 40' rock-climbing wall, speed and heavy boxing bags, a martial arts studio—and all the free weights, fitness equipment, and exercise classes you'd ever want. The club also has a restaurant and cafe, along with services such as dry cleaning, tailoring, shoe repair, hair styling, and day care. It is all marble and carpets and wood paneling and great towels. Every time the elevator opens it seems as though yet another celebrity has arrived.

Chelsea Piers (212-336-6500) West 23rd Street at the West Side Hwy

This 30-acre, $100 million, privately financed project transformed four neglected West Side piers into an amazing sports and entertainment complex. At Chelsea Piers you will find restaurants, shops, a marina, film and sound stage, and photography studios. The facility also contains the following: a 150,000 square-foot sports and fitness center, a boxing ring, indoor NHL-regulation size and Olympic-size ice skating rinks, and two outdoor in-line and roller skating rinks. It also provides a four-tier golf driving range with 200-yard fairway, a gymnastics training center, two indoor artificial-turf fields for soccer and lacrosse, three basketball/volleyball courts, two hardwood hoops courts, a huge swimming pool, and batting cages. The most recent addition is a state-of-the-art bowling center. Although I haven't heard any rumors about elephant polo yet, there might very well be miniature golf on a barge in the river. Some activities are members-only and others are pay-as-you-go.

Deciding Where to Play

Where you decide to play sports is likely motivated by a long list of considerations that includes location, cost, programs, and personal taste. Private clubs with higher fees usually have more equipment, more programs, and more comfortable surroundings. Visit first before making a decision. What one person might see as old and cramped, another might view as charming and cozy; what one person might consider state-of-the-art, another might judge cold and sterile. One person might prefer the company of a variety of people, another might complain that "there just aren't enough people like *me*."

Call First

Nothing in New York stays the same for very long, so make it a policy to call before you visit any of the facilities listed here. A simple phone call can also yield some valuable information about costs, memberships, schedules, hours of operation, travel directions, and program offerings that vary from month to month and season to season.

Watching

Some basic information about New York's major professional teams has been included here, but don't overlook the minor league clubs or colleges and universities that are also listed. Both the minor leaguers and the college kids are fun to watch. They play the game hard, and they play it

pure. As for the colleges, although the strength of their sports programs often vary from year to year, St. John's hoops is almost always strong. And if you can get to a Big East tournament game at the Garden with St. John's still in the hunt for a championship, it just doesn't get any more exciting. The phone numbers listed for the colleges will put you in touch with the Sports Information Office, which can provide you with schedules, locations, and directions.

Surfing the Net

There's a wealth of sports information available through the Internet. Here are two of the best New York oriented sites:

New York Sports Online
http://www.nynow.com/nysol/

NYSOL not only features stories about New York's professional sports teams and has links to other sites of interest, but is the only website dedicated to recreational, amateur, and participatory sports in the tri-state area. The homepage offers feature stories, news and events for the week. Choose from almost 40 individual listings ranging from the familiar (baseball, soccer, basketball, football, hockey, golf, tennis) to the less familiar (climbing, cricket, sailing, lacrosse) to the really unfamiliar (netball, fencing, handball, hurling, sky diving).

MetroSport Magazine
http://www.metrosports.com/

This website focuses on running, cycling, in-line skating, skiing, racquet sports, water sports, fitness, triathlon, outdoor adventure, and volleyball. From the homepage, you can click on the sport of your choice to get news and events. *MetroSport* has affiliations with skating and running associations in nearby cities that let you keep tabs on events in Boston, Connecticut, Philadelphia, and Washington D.C. The hard copy is free and can be found at area gyms and at book and sporting goods stores.

So What Are You Waiting For?

Read *Sports New York* and learn about where you can play, learn, and watch over 75 different sports. Choose the ones you like, then get outside and get going!

Steve Schwartz
New York City, 1998

Sports is the only profession I know that when you retire, you have to go to work.

—EARL MONROE, former New York Knick

1
SPORTS
with
ARGUING
and
CHEERING

BASEBALL AND SOFTBALL

If a woman has to choose between catching a fly ball and saving an infant's life, she will choose to save the infant's life without even considering if there are men on base. —DAVE BARRY, humorist

THERE ARE 134 PUBLIC BASEBALL AND SOFTBALL DIAMONDS IN MANHATTAN, and you can play regularly on any of them by getting a permit from the Manhattan Borough Office (212-408-0209), 16 West 61st Street, between Broadway and 9th Avenue. This office is open from 9 to 5 during the week. Your best bet is to go in person since the number is often busy. If you're interested in a non-Manhattan site, call the borough office where the field is located.

Playing and Watching

These are good places for pickup games after work and on the weekends in-season:

CENTRAL PARK

The Great Lawn
Mid-Central Park at about 83rd Street
Eight fields.

Hecksher Fields
Mid-Central Park at about 62nd Street
Five fields.

North Meadow
Mid-Central Park at about 97th Street
12 fields, one lit for night play.

Riverbank State Park (212-694-3600)
Hudson River at 145th Street
Has a beautiful artificial turf baseball/softball field with lights. It is open from the beginning of March to the end of October. Although many community league games are played here, pick-up games are not uncommon.

Riverside Park
On the Hudson River at 75th Street, 102nd, 103rd, 104th, 107th, and 108th
One field at each location.

Leagues

Carmine Recreation Center
(212-242-5228)
Clarkson Street and 7th Avenue South
Has leagues for both men and women. Games are played on a well-kept field, directly behind the center and smack in the middle of a concrete, glass, and steel cityscape. It looks like a New York set of *Field of Dreams*, and quite the sight when lit for night play. To reserve the field, call the Manhattan Borough office at 212-408-0209.

Central Park Softball League
(212-765-0771)
Plays a 25-game schedule on weekdays and Saturdays at Hecksher Fields. Their season runs

from April to September, and, although some women participate, this isn't considered a coed league. The league plays modified fast-pitch and is competitive. Call early to reserve a spot. If you get Morty Gilbert on the phone, you're in luck because he knows the local softball scene better than anybody else.

Corporate Sports (212-245-4738)

Runs coed, men's, and women's slow and modified fast-pitch leagues. All have 12-game schedules and run from mid-April through mid-August. Games are played on weekday evenings at various fields around town. Since you can't sign up on an individual basis, you'll need to round up a group of friends and enter a team. Teams are placed in a division with others of similar strength.

New York Women's Baseball League (718-748-8823)

Originated by pioneer Connie White, this is the only league of its kind in the Northeast. The NYWBL adheres to Major League Baseball rules and sponsors a ten-game season that runs from June to September. The league attracts both those with prior baseball experience as well as former softball standouts. There are tryouts in May. Weekly practices are held in Brooklyn, and games take place in New York and other cities on the weekends.

New York Women's Sports League (Jean Silva at 718-544-7436).

This league has been in operation for over 20 years and has a May to August softball season of 15 to 18 games, including playoffs and an All-Star game. There is also a September to November season of ten to 12 games. They play once a week in the early evenings on a field under the Manhattan Bridge (at Market and Monroe Streets). You can either join as an individual (team managers are always looking for players) or as a team.

Women Athletes of New York (212-759-4189)

A nonprofit organization founded in 1981 with approximately 400 female members involved in various sports. Team managers are always looking for experienced players, so don't hesitate to try out. You can also enter a team. The season runs from the first weekend in May to the beginning of September, and consists of 16 games, plus playoffs. Games are played in Manhattan and Astoria, Queens.

Yorkville Sports Association (212-645-6488) http://home.earthlink.net/~ysa/

Conducts men's, women's, and coed softball leagues from April to August, and *snowflake* softball beginning in September. There are 13 games plus playoffs and an All Star game. Games are played in the early evening at various fields in Manhattan. You can enter a team or sign up as an individual. Individuals attend an open scrimmage and are placed on teams based on their ability.

Tournaments

The city-wide Mayor's Cup softball tournament is held every August and September. It begins with borough-by-borough qualifying games leading up to playoffs and a championship game. There are men's and women's modified fast-pitch divisions, and a coed division that plays slow pitch. For an application or information about schedules and locations, call the New York City Sports Commission at 212-788-8389.

Batting Cages

Chelsea Piers (212-336-6500)
West 23rd Street at the West Side Hwy

Four baseball and softball cages, each with variable speeds for lefties and righties.

Coney Island Batting Range (718-449-1200)
3049 Stillwell Avenue between Surf and the Boardwalk

Even though Coney Island is a far cry from what it was in its heyday, it remains a fascinating part of our cultural history and is absolutely worth a visit. On summer weekends it's crowded, noisy, and vibrant, and if it takes these nine outdoor cages to get you to visit, great. And by the way, they're just down the street from the original Nathan's.

Gateway Sports Center (718-253-6816)
3200 Flatbush Avenue, Brooklyn

This facility is opposite Floyd Bennett Field and is a real schlepp without a car. But there are 12 outdoor cages here (seven baseball and five softball). There's also a snack bar in case the trip made you hungry. And if you have any energy left after swinging the bat, don't overlook the driving range, miniature golf, and tennis courts.

Hackers, Hitters, & Hoops (212-929-7492)
123 West 18th Street between 6th and 7th Avenues

A sports and entertainment bar with food, drinks, and various sports activities, including a small hoops court, and two variable-speed baseball/softball batting cages.

Randall's Island Family Golf Center (212-427-5689)

Here you'll find nine batting cages, six for baseball (two each for slow, medium, and fast. One of these is *really* fast—87 mph at 42 feet), and three for softball. Randall's Island itself is some 400 acres of tennis courts, baseball and soccer fields, and more. It is surprising how quiet and far away this place seems from the hustle and bustle of Manhattan, but it is easily accessible by public transportation or shuttle van (call the above number for a schedule) that first departs from Manhattan in the late afternoon.

Turtle Cove Golf Complex (718-885-2646)
1 City Island Road at Shore Road, City Island

Nine outdoor cages: five baseball (from Little League to Triple A speed) and four softball (slow, medium, fast, arc). It's a subway and bus ride to get here, but City Island itself is well worth the trek, boasting Victorian houses, marinas, sailing schools, trinket shops, and some excellent seafood. Try Johnny's Reef (718-885-2036), a fast-food/fried-food restaurant with waterside picnic tables. For a sit-down meal, consider the Lobster Box (718-885-1952) 34 City Island Avenue, at Belden, which has superb views of Long Island Sound from almost anywhere in the dining room.

Pro Ball

Mets (718-507-8499)
Shea Stadium, Flushing, Queens
http://www.mets.com

Tickets for all but the most important games are generally available and can be purchased by phone or at the box office.

Yankees (718-293-6000)
Yankee Stadium, the Bronx
http://www.yankees.com

The Yankees have enjoyed regular success over the years, so it's good that Yankee Stadium is quite large and there are *lots* of games. To purchase tickets, call or visit the stadium. Tickets are available also in midtown at the Yankee Clubhouse Shop's two locations (110 E. 59th Street between Park and Lexington Avenues, 758-7844; and 393 Fifth Avenue between 36th and 37th Streets, 685-4693) for a $3 service charge per ticket.

Minor League Ball

Hudson Valley Renegades
(914-838-0094)
Duchess County Stadium,
Wappinger's Falls, NY

The Renegades (Class A, affiliated with the Texas Rangers) play on a June to September schedule. The stadium is about a 1-1/2 hour drive from Manhattan.

New Jersey Cardinals (973-579-7500)

Skylands Park, Sussex County, NJ
The Cardinals (Class A, St. Louis Cardinals) play a June to September schedule. Skylands Park is 55 miles from the George Washington Bridge.

Trenton Thunder (609-394-TEAM)
Mercer County Waterfront Park,
Trenton, NJ

The Thunder (Double A, Boston Red Sox) play a June to September schedule. The park is about 1-1/2 hours by car, bus, or train, and is a terrific place to watch a game.

College Ball

Columbia University (Manhattan)
212-854-2546 (men's baseball/women's softball)
Fordham University (the Bronx)
718-817-4240 (men's baseball)
Long Island University (Brooklyn) 718-488-1240
(men's baseball and women's softball)
St. John's University (Queens) 718-990-6367
(men's baseball/women's softball)
Wagner College (Staten Island) 718-390-3227
(men's baseball/women's softball)

Did you know?

That the first recorded baseball game ever played was on June 9, 1846, at Hoboken's Elysian Fields? The New York Club defeated the Knickerbockers 23-1, and Davis, the winning pitcher, was fined 50 cents for swearing at an umpire.

That in 1867, a Brooklyn pitcher named William Arthur Cummings threw the first recorded curve ball?

That the Brooklyn Dodgers got their name because of all the trolley cars that pedestrians had to avoid while trying to cross Brooklyn streets?

That during the first game played in the Polo Grounds (August 19, 1917) Giants' manager John McGraw and Reds' manager Christy Mathewson were arrested for playing ball on Sunday?

That Boston Red Sox owner Harry Frazee sold a young player to the Yankees in order to bankroll the Broadway show *No, No Nanette?* One hundred thousand dollars brought Babe Ruth to New York in 1920. Ain't show biz grand?

BASKETBALL

The ability to rebound is inversely proportional to the distance one grew up from the railroad tracks. —PETE CARRIL, former Princeton University basketball coach.

SCHOOLYARD HOOPS IN NEW YORK IS ABOUT ATTITUDE AND TALENT, attitude and jump shooting, attitude and arguing, attitude and hard work, and just plain attitude. There's not much defense except for shot blocking and no easy passes when a behind-the-back-look-away will do. The closest it ever gets to a "pick and roll" is "ham on a roll" from the nearest deli. You'd better be ready if you want to play, or else you'll have to take a seat along the fence with the rest of the losers.

Also, every schoolyard has its own rules: rules about getting into games (*Who's got next?* is pretty standard), about fouls (*no blood, no foul* usually works), and rules about taking the ball behind the line after misses. So watch a little first, prepare to be ignored for a while, then go for it.

Pickup Games and Leagues:
Indoors and Outdoors

Asphalt Green (212-369-8890, Ext. 114)
555 East 90th Street at York Avenue
One indoor and two outdoor full courts. The indoor court is in a cramped gym, but the two outdoors are right alongside the FDR Drive. It's a terrific feeling to be shooting hoops while the rush-hour traffic does its bumper-to-bumper thing. There are men's summer and winter leagues that play eight-game plus playoff schedules. These leagues are only open to teams. There is also coed free play on various nights of the week. Call for information on membership plans.

Basketball City (212-924-4040)
West 23rd Street at the West Side Hwy
Over 30,000 air-conditioned square feet containing six indoor courts with electronic backboards, men's and women's locker rooms, a fitness center, and a lounge. There are also 12 outdoor half-courts open seasonally and for special events. You can join Basketball City as an individual or as a team, and participate in one of their weeknight or weekend leagues. Corporate leagues, for example, include 12-game seasons plus playoffs, team shirts, referees, scorekeeper, and statistician. The facility also offers three-on-three tourneys, instructional clinics, and one-on-one training. This is a membership-only facility, although you can pay a guest fee and bring along a friend. New members are rated according to ability, so you will always get to play games with people at your own level. If you're serious about your hoops, check this out.

Carl Schurz Park
84th Street and East End Avenue
Has three cramped half courts. The games are

usually fairly laid back—but beware of the roller hockey players who occasionally drift over from the adjacent rink.

Central Park
Around 86th Street, near the Metropolitan Museum of Art
Has two full courts with mixed-ability levels.

Chelsea Piers (212-366-6500)
West 23rd Street at the West Side Hwy
Men's, women's, and coed leagues year-round in four categories: recreational, intermediate, competitive, and over-30. You can join as an individual or as a team. The season consists of ten games plus playoffs. And if you aren't the organized league type, Chelsea also offers free play and pickup games. Plus, if you're really antisocial, you can rent one of their two hardwood courts just for yourself.

Corporate Sports (212-245-4738)
Offers men's, women's, and coed leagues throughout the year, with games played at various Manhattan high school gyms. The winter league plays 14 games (the first week of November through the end of February) and the spring league plays ten games (mid-April through the end of June). Games are played one night a week, and although they're serious, the level of competition varies. You can't join this league as an individual, so start recruiting some buddies. Each team is placed in a division with others of similar ability.

Greater New York Pro-Am
(212-636-5020)
Runs summer and winter leagues for men and women at various locations, and attracts very high-caliber players. NBA stars Anthony Mason, Chris Mullin, and Rod Strickland are league alumnae. You can join the league with a team or enter as an individual. Coaches recruit players, and tryouts are required. Call for current information and application forms.

Hamilton Fish Recreation Center (212-387-6788)
128 Pitt Street, at Houston
Two outdoor courts with free play and a summer men's league.

McBurney YMCA (212-741-9210)
215 West 23rd between 7th and 8th Avenues
Year-round free play and a men's league in the winter. League registration begins December 1st and play begins at the end of January.

New York Urban Professional's Athletic League (212-877-3614)
Teams or individuals can join this league, which boasts over 375 teams in 23 divisions. There are women's and men's leagues for winter and summer play. Unaffiliated individuals are placed on a team (with players of comparable skill) during an open scrimmage. The games are played in public and private school gyms all over Manhattan with a 12-game schedule (eight in the summer), plus divisional and interdivisional playoffs. In addition to winter and summer schedules, there's also fall and spring three-on-three. The league draws professional people ranging in age from 20 to 50, and also organizes clinics, open

play, and numerous social events (parties, cruises, and comedy-night outings).

New York Women's Sports League (call Jean Silva at 718-544-7436)
This league has been in operation for over 20 years and plays 12 to 15 games during the season. The games are played once a week in the Chinatown area. Teams and individuals are welcome, and team managers are always looking for players.

94th Street and Madison Avenue
In the Armory courtyard. Has three full courts and mixed-ability levels.

92nd Street Y (212-415-5700)
1395 Lexington Avenue at 92nd Street
Has a men's league that plays October through January. One night of the week is reserved for those who have entered with a team, and another for those who have joined as individuals. There are two nights reserved for free play: one for women, another for coed.

Reebok (212-362-6800)
160 Columbus Avenue between 67th and 68th Streets
Two full courts, plus two half courts for in-house leagues and free play. There's an A and B league based on ability level, and both are very competitive. During their first year, the New York Liberty of the WNBA used Reebok as their practice site. I'm 6'4", an ex-jock, and was very happy to have survived a three-on-three with these women with the small shred of ego I had left.

Riverbank State Park (212-694-3600)
Hudson River at 145th Street
Has a beautiful gym with views of the Hudson, bleachers that sit 1,000 people, and three full courts. There is open play during the week and on weekends, as well as the Old Timers Open Gym on Sunday evenings for anyone who is over 30. There are also four outdoor courts, which are open from the beginning of April to the end of December. The level of play here is relatively high, so be prepared to sit if you can't keep up.

Riverside Park At 76th, 103rd and 110th Streets
Has competitive full court games with the West Side Highway and Hudson River as a backdrop, at 76th and 103rd Streets, and several half courts at 110th Street.

West 4th Street and Avenue of the Americas
Has a short court with very good players. There's almost always an audience, and it's often a dunk-a-thon. Better be ready. There's also a West 4th Street summer league with professional-amateur, youth, and women's divisions. It runs mid-June to mid-August. Call Kenneth Graham (718-875-2947) for more information.

West 76th Street and Columbus Avenue
Has six half courts, uneven surfaces, and an Upper West Side crowd that mixes Air Jordans and Bierkenstocks. The schoolyard is always closed on Sundays for a flea market.

West Side Y (212-787-4400)
5 West 63rd Street between Central Park West and Broadway
Offers a league for members and nonmembers that runs from January to April—including playoffs and a championship game. The entry fee covers referees, awards, and a T-shirt. There are also nights for free play—plus a women-only night.

Women Athletes of New York (212-759-4189)

Runs a league from October to January with games played in various Manhattan locations. This isn't a league for absolute beginners. Teams and individuals are welcome to join.

Yorkville Sports Association (212-645-6488) http://home.earthlink.net/~ysa/

Runs men's and women's basketball leagues during the winter and spring seasons. Players must be 21 or older, and if you're not entering with a team, you can attend an open scrimmage where new ones are formed. The spring/summer season is seven games long, plus playoffs, and all games are played in Manhattan gyms. Yorkville also has open play nights.

YWCA (212-755-2700) 610 Lexington Avenue at 53rd Street

Not only is this *YWCA* coed like all the *YMCAs* are, it runs men's basketball leagues during all four seasons. The fall and spring leagues have nine-game schedules, the winter eight, the summer seven. The entry fee (for either teams or individuals) includes refs, T-shirts, trophies, and free use of the facility's fitness center on specific days of the week. If you want to join the league as an individual, you are either placed on a team comprised totally of "walk-ons," or on one of the existing teams that needs a player. In addition to the leagues, there are scheduled free play sessions.

Pro Hoops

Knicks (212-465-6741) Madison Square Garden, 7th Avenue between 31st and 33rd Streets http://www.nba.com/knicks

Since it's almost impossible to buy Knicks tickets, you're left with two options: get invited by someone, or buy from a scalper, which is against the law and very expensive (beware of counterfeit tickets). If you've never done this before, just stand around looking forlorn, and you'll be approached in the blink of an eye.

Liberty (212-465-6073) Madison Square Garden, 7th Avenue between 31st and 33rd Streets http://www.wnba.com/liberty/

Tickets for New York's professional women's team can be purchased at the Garden box office, or by calling Ticketmaster at 212-307-7171. For season tickets, call 212-465-6073. The WNBA season runs from June to August, with 14 home games at the Garden.

Nets (201-935-8888) Continental Arena, East Rutherford, NJ http://www.nba.com/nets

Going to a Nets game can usually be a last-minute decision because tickets are almost always available. Call to reserve or go directly to the box office. New Jersey Transit buses from the Port Authority (973-762-5100) will get you to the arena and back.

College Hoops

Columbia University (Manhattan) 212-854-2546
Fordham University (the Bronx) 718-817-4240
Long Island University (Brooklyn) 718-488-1240
Manhattan College (the Bronx) 718-862-7227
New York University (Manhattan) 212-998-2029
St. John's University (Queens) 718-990-6367
Wagner College (Staten Island) 718-390-3227

In-Line Basketball

The National In-line Basketball League (212-539-1132)
http://www.nibbl.com

Founded by former player Tom LaGarde in 1993, the NIBL features fast skating, three-point and four-point shots, an 18-second clock, and amazing skill. There are currently teams in New York, New Jersey, Connecticut, Boston, Toronto, and Puerto Rico. The season, which runs from mid-April to early October, features an All-Star game and championship tournament. Games are played in Tompkins and Union Square Parks and are really something to see.

> **Did you know?**
> **That on February 17, 1963, a guy named Michael Jordan was born in Brooklyn, New York?**

BOCCIE

Basketball's not my sport. Boccie ball's my sport.
It's a gentleman's sport. You don't have to run around like an animal.
—FATHER GUIDO SARDUCCI, comic television cleric

THE DICTIONARY DEFINES BOCCIE AS: "A game of Italian origin similar to bowling that is played with wooden balls on a long, narrow court covered with fine gravel." Well, that's true as far as it goes, but what it leaves out completely is the emotion, intensity, and *passion* this game arouses. Boccie is played by primarily Italian men—mostly elderly, enormously competitive and argumentative, always gesticulating—and usually chain-smoking.

By the way, the French play a boccie-like game called *petanque.* Instead of rolling wooden balls down an alley-type affair to score points and knock opponents out of position, players use steel balls, and *loft* them in the air to do the same things. And if you're still not clear about who the French (playing petanque) are and who the Italians (playing boccie) are, you really have to get out more.

Playing and Watching

The Bronx
Van Cortlandt Park East at 233rd Street

Brooklyn
Marine Park, Fillmore and Garrison Beach at Avenue U

Manhattan
Stanley Isaacs Playground, East 95th Street and the FDR Drive
Robert Moses Playground, East 41st Street

and 1st Avenue
Thompson Street Playground, Thompson and Houston Street
James J. Walker Park, Hudson Street, between Leroy and Clarkson Street
Carmine Recreation Center (212-242-5228) Clarkson Street and 7th Avenue South

Queens
Juniper Valley Park, Juniper Valley Road North, at 79th

Staten Island
South Beach, Father Capodano Boccie Court, Doti and Linda Streets

Playing and Watching and Eating: Indoors

Il Vagabondo Restaurant (212-832-9221)
351 East 62nd Street between 1st and 2nd Avenues

Il Vagabondo is half Northern Italian Restaurant with reasonable prices and decent food, and half boccie court. Eat veal and pasta, drink red wine, and play boccie. So what could be bad?

Playing and Watching and Eating: Outdoors

Play at Corona Avenue and 108th Street in Queens, and eat at the Parkside Restaurant right across the street. And again, so what could be bad?

City Tournament

This usually takes place over the Columbus Day weekend, beginning with borough-by-borough qualifiers on Saturday (over 100 teams participate), and concluding on Sunday with finals in Brooklyn's Marine Park (Fillmore and Garrison Beach, at Avenue U). If you think the Super Bowl is it for intensity, you should check out this tournament. Call 212-360-8222 for locations and schedules.

GYMNASTICS

It's hard to find heels that don't have Mickey Mouse on them.

—BRANDY JOHNSON, gymnast on trying to find size 3 shoes

IN 1832, IT WAS FEARED THAT CITY LIVING WAS CAUSING PHYSICAL DETERIORATION IN WOMEN. Newspapers of the time considered gentle calisthenics a remedy, and inserted illustrations of various exercises, hoping their readers would take the hint. If urban life over 160 years ago was causing women to deteriorate, can you imagine what's happening to us today? And if *gentle calisthenics* were the cure then, maybe our only hope today is gymnastics.

Playing and Learning

Asphalt Green (212-369-8890)
555 East 90th Street at York Avenue
Offers a package of 15 classes that utilizes all of their gymnastics apparatus, and emphasizes strength, flexibility, and coordination.

Chelsea Piers (212-336-6500)
West 23rd Street at the West Side Hwy
Has a 23,000 square-foot gymnastics center with a ton of gear: from beams, rings, horses, and vaults to in-ground trampolines, deep-foam training pits, tumble tracks, and two column-free competition spring floors. The area is huge and bright, the ceiling is high, and the site is sanctioned by USA Gymnastics for local, state, and regional competitions. All instructors are safety-certified, and beginner to elite classes are offered on an ongoing basis.

Drago's Gymnasium (212-757-0724)
50 West 57th Street between 5th and 6th Avenues
Offers private, semiprivate, and group lessons on their mats, rings, trapeze, and parallel bars. The semiprivate classes are limited to six students. The first 20 minutes are warm-up, followed by individualized instruction. The emphasis at Drago's isn't on preparation for the Olympics, but rather at working at your own pace and developing a well-conditioned body.

Wendy Hilliard (212-721-3256)
166 West 92nd Street at Amsterdam Avenue, in the Central Baptist Church
Offers classes in rhythmic gymnastics. Wendy is a nine-time national team member, a four-time national team coach, and a national and international gold medalist. If rhythmic gymnastics sounds familiar but you can't quite place it, it's that graceful and beautiful sport you've seen on TV that combines dance, gymnastics, and a variety of paraphernalia (jump ropes, hoops, balls, Indian clubs, elegant long ribbons). Wendy offers adult classes for men and women. For $15 you can give the sport a try before registering.

McBurney YMCA (212-741-9210)
215 West 23rd Street between 7th and 8th Avenues
Offers instruction on a wide range of apparatus, including pommel horse, uneven and parallel bars, balance beam, rings, vault, mats, and tumble track.

Sutton Gymnastics and Fitness Center (212-533-9390)
20 Cooper Square between Lafayette and 3rd Avenue
Features a strong complement of equipment, including rings, high bar, vault, pommel horse, uneven bars, parallel bars, balance beam, trampoline, tumble track, and a 3,400 square foot competition spring-floor. Private and semiprivate classes are available for men and women at beginner, intermediate, and advanced levels.

NETBALL

THIS GAME STARTED IN BOSTON SOMETIME AROUND 1891, migrated to England, and today is played in over 50 countries and on every continent. It is very well known almost everywhere except in the U.S., and, although men play as well, it is currently the world's most popular game for women. The sport will be showcased at the 2000 Olympic Games in Sydney, Australia.

Netball is played seven to a side, and involves throwing a ball into something similar to a basketball hoop that is attached to a post—but without any backboard. No physical contact is allowed, and players have to pass or shoot within three seconds. As in basketball, they can take only a limited number of steps.

Although there are club teams, they are very informal. Games are held on Saturday or Sunday afternoons in the summer. Call Ava Foster (718-341-1432), the Development Director for the New York Region, for more information.

Locations

Brooklyn: Harry Maze Park, East 56th between Clarendon Road and Avenue D

The Bronx: Agnes Haywood Park, 216th Street and Barnes Avenue

STICKBALL

FOR MANY OF US WHO GREW UP IN THE BRONX, stickball was life. It was played with a cut-down broom handle and a Spalding ball. Fire hydrants and parked cars marked the playing field, and hits were measured by how many sewers a ball passed on the fly. The rules varied a little depending on your neighborhood, but the basics were always the same: Smack the ball and run like hell until you were tagged out, thrown out, or a fielder hit you with the ball. Have you ever seen the famous picture of Willie Mays playing stickball with a bunch of kids? Willie was a classic, and the game still is.

Playing and Watching

Bronx All-Stars
Behind Roosevelt High School, Fordham Road and Bathgate Avenue
These guys play the best regular pickup game in late spring, summer, and early fall on Sundays at 8 AM.

Daily News Stickball Tournament
Cosponsored by the city, the tourney runs from the end of June to the beginning of September. It's a five-borough affair that involves eight-player teams and various long-ball hitting contests.

Look for ads in the newspaper around midsummer.

111th Street Oldtimers Stickball Association Annual Celebration
111th Street and Fifth Avenue
Held on the second Sunday of July. If you want to play, get there early and write your name on the sidewalk. A celebrity All-Star game takes place at 10 AM, followed by food, music, and partying until well after 8 PM. A note of caution: Be careful of all the "old guys" walking around with bats in their hands—yes, they're playing with their sons and even grandsons and they aren't as young as they once were—but trust me, they're still young enough to kick your ass.

VOLLEYBALL

Twenty-two people on the beach who quit playing when the hamburgers are ready. —STEVE TIMMONS, pro volleyball player commenting on how most people view his sport

VOLLEYBALL WAS INVENTED IN 1895 BY WILLIAM MORGAN OF THE MT. HOLYOKE, Massachusetts YMCA, who taught exercise classes for businessmen. He couldn't find a less strenuous game than basketball that would also eliminate physical contact so he invented one. Originally, the game was called *mintonette* and used a basketball. I imagine the first few sprained wrists and broken fingers made him realize the ball was way too heavy, so he asked the Spalding company to design a new one. Since volleyball was invented to be kinder and gentler than hoops, and since our modern version is in *no way* kind and *no way* gentle, it would be interesting to see what the game looked like when Morgan rolled the first ball onto the court.

There is a variation of volleyball called *walleyball* that is played on a squash or racquetball court with two teams and a net. The ball is playable off the walls, thus, walleyball. But you know, I just can't deal with this game. The name sounds too much like an unwatchable Chevy Chase movie.

Playing

Carmine Recreation Center
(212-242-5228)
Clarkson Street and 7th Avenue South
Drop-in coed volleyball for beginning, intermediate, and advanced players, with different nights for each. Instruction for beginners and intermediates is also offered.

Central Park

Mid-park at 68th Street (three courts), mid-park around 86th Street (two courts)

To obtain a court permit send a SASE to Parks and Recreation, Permits Office, 16 West 61st Street, NYC 10023. There is no cost for the permit, but remember it's BYOB(AN), bring your own ball and net.

McBurney YMCA (212-741-9210)
215 West 23rd Street between 7th and 8th Avenues

Groups players according to ability level and sets aside specific days so that people with similar skills can play pickup games. There is also a night of open play when anyone can show up.

Riverbank State Park (212-634-3600)
Hudson River at 145th Street

Open volleyball on various nights of the week. Call for a schedule.

West Side Y (212-787-4400)
5 West 63rd Street between Central Park West and Broadway

Typically offers open volleyball two nights a week, with one night for beginning players and the other for intermediate and up.

Leagues

Big City Volleyball League (212-288-4240)

Plays men's, women's, and coed games at Upper East and West Side locations. Big City runs leagues four times a year. Each season lasts three months and includes ten professionally reffed games plus playoffs. The league is divided into seven levels that range from absolute beginner to college level. Members get a T-shirt, biweekly newsletter, and discounts at local restaurants.

Chelsea Piers (212-336-6000)
The Sports Center
West 23rd Street at the West Side Hwy

Coed league plays one night a week, and free play is available every night.

New York Urban Professional's Athletic League (212-877-3614)

This league features over 250 teams in 22 men's, women's, and coed divisions. Play takes place during fall, winter, and spring seasons. Teams and individuals can join; individuals are placed on a team with players of similar ability during an open scrimmage. The games take place in public and private school gyms all over Manhattan, and the season includes ten games (eight in the summer) plus divisional and interdivisional playoffs. The league draws professional people in the 20-50-year-old range, and also organizes clinics, open play, and numerous social events.

New York Women's Sports League (Jean Silva at 718-544-7436)

The season lasts 12 to 15 games that are played one night a week in the Chinatown area. Both individuals and teams are welcome.

Reebok (212-362-6800) 160 Columbus Avenue between 67th and 68th Streets

Offers open volleyball in the gym for members and guests. There is also an in-house league during the season.

V League (212-721-1470)

Coed league with five divisions based on skill level (beginning to college players). The season runs eight games plus playoffs. Individuals and teams can sign up. Games are played Monday through Thursday, and teams play on the same night and in the same gym. Prizes are awarded for division winners and runners-up. There is also a social element here with parties and discounts at various bars.

Vanderbilt YMCA (212-756-9600) 224 East 47th Street between 2nd and 3rd Avenues

Instruction is available for men and women at all skill levels. The Y also runs winter and spring leagues.

Women Athletes of New York (212-759-4189)

The volleyball season runs from mid-November to the beginning of April and consists of about 13 games, plus playoffs. Games are played in Manhattan locations, and the level of competition is high. Both teams and individuals can join.

Yorkville Sports Association (212-645-6488) http://home.earthlink.net/~ysa/

Runs men's, women's, and coed leagues during the winter and spring with 11-game schedules, plus playoffs and an All-Star game. Games are played at various high schools in Manhattan. Enter a team, or sign up as an individual. Individuals are placed on teams with other players at the same level after an open scrimmage. Yorkville also runs a professional league comprised of pro, AA, and open-level players. This season begins in October and games are held at the Hunter College gym (68th Street and Lexington Avenue).

YWCA (212-755-2700) 610 Lexington Avenue at 53rd Street

Runs coed volleyball leagues that you can join as an individual or with a team. Individuals are placed on a team with other "walk-ons," or on an existing team that needs a player.

Tournaments

Mayor's Cup Volleyball Tournament

Played at various sites in Manhattan over one weekend in March or April. There are five divisions for men and women. For information about schedules and locations, call the New York City Sports Commission at 212-788-8389.

City-Wide Sand Volleyball Tournament (212-360-8222)

Attracting some 200 teams, the tourney is held every year in mid-July. It begins with borough-by-borough qualifiers and concludes with finals on the beach in Coney Island. The Manhattan qualifying matches are held in Central Park.

So Who Needs California?

New York City has its own sand volleyball courts. One is located in mid-Central Park at around 68th Street. Another is at Chelsea Piers. They trucked in 190 tons of sand to make this court, and offer a league to go along with it. There are three others on Pier 25, at North Moore Street, five blocks south of Canal. These courts are outside and lit for night play. There are leagues and tournaments, or you can arrange to play with a group of friends. Call 212-571-2323 for costs, schedules, and reservations. The courts were built by the *Hudson River Conservancy* (212-533-PARK), which was formed by the state and city to design, build, and operate a waterfront park extending from Battery Park to 59th Street.

College Volleyball (Women):

Fordham University (the Bronx)
718-817-4240

Long Island University (Brooklyn)
718-488-1240

St. John's University (Queens)
718-990-6367

Wagner College (Staten Island)
718-390-3227

2

SPORTS with ARGUING, BETTING, and CHEERING

HORSE RACING

I bet on a horse at ten to one. It didn't come in until half-past five.

—HENNY YOUNGMAN, comedian

I WENT TO AQUEDUCT YEARS AGO WITH THREE FRIENDS, all of whom were over 60, and any of whom could have stepped out of a Broadway production of *Guys and Dolls.* Warren was a private investigator with a frayed collar and an old .38 in a shoulder holster. Murray was a degenerate gambler who somehow wound up running an OTB parlor. And Jack was a writer and journalist who had grown up on a horse farm in Kentucky. Each guy had played the horses for over 40 years and considered himself an expert. And each had his own source at the track: guys who were wired into the *sure things.*

When we arrived, Warren went to Tony the Bartender, Murray to Johnny the Groom, and Jack to Phil the Headwaiter. As 120 combined years of betting expertise went to consult with three guys in the know, I stayed back to decide how to spend all the money I was going to make. Then everyone returned with the "supposed" winner of the first race:

Warren said, "The seven horse."
"The three horse," Murray declared.
And Jack proclaimed, "The nine horse."

All three of the "sure thing" guys had a different horse. And not only that, but Murray disagreed with Johnny the Groom. He was convinced that the four horse had the best shot. And Jack said Phil the Headwaiter blew this one. Jack was adamant that the eight couldn't be beat. So there I stood with five winners for the first race. Did I win it? No. Did my friends continue to consult and disagree? Yes. I win anything? Sure. Nine bucks total for the day, and this great story.

"Playing" and Watching

Aqueduct (718-641-4700) Rockaway Boulevard and 108th Street, Ozone Park, Queens

The winter season runs from late October to mid-May. Aqueduct opened in 1894, was torn down in 1956, and then was rebuilt as the *Big A,* a modern thoroughbred racetrack with a capacity of about 85,000 and lovely lawns and gardens. But if you're looking at the lovely lawns and gardens, you ain't betting. And if you ain't betting, why are you there?

Belmont Park (718-641-4700) Hempstead Turnpike, Elmont, Long Island

Belmont, established in 1905, is the home of the Belmont Stakes, the third jewel in the Triple Crown. The season here splits mid-May through mid-July, then September through mid-October. Belmont has a capacity of 90,000 people, sprawls across some 450 acres, and has beautifully manicured lawns, special Sunday breakfasts, and tram rides around the grounds. But if you're looking at lawns, eating breakfast, or taking tram rides, you ain't betting. And if you ain't betting, why are you there? Historical note: In 1910, an international aerial tournament was staged there, supervised by none other than the Wright Brothers.

Meadowlands Race Track (201-935-8500) East Rutherford, NJ

Harness racing takes place from the end of December to mid-August, then thoroughbred racing takes over from September to mid-December. The track opened in 1976 for harness racing, and three years later, began its 100-day thoroughbred meet. The Meadowlands has a one-mile oval, and a capacity of about 40,000. New Jersey Transit buses will get you there from the Port Authority (973-762-5100). Since the Meadowlands isn't as pretty as Aqueduct or Belmont, there isn't much to keep you from making a few bets.

Yonkers Raceway (914-968-4200) Yonkers, New York

The modern raceway had its inaugural meet in 1950, but the original track dates back to the 19th century when it was founded to replace Fleetwood Park in the Bronx. Yonkers is now up for sale, but harness racing still takes place year-round. The track, a half-mile oval, accommodates some 7,500 people in its current configuration. Yonkers is about eight miles from Yankee Stadium and is accessible by subway and bus. You know, this is a place where you probably *should* look around a little; there's just no telling how long it will stay with us.

Did you know?

That in 1664, horse racing became the first organized sport in the country when New York State's governor, Richard Nicolls, established a track in Hempstead Plain, Long Island? It was called the Newmarket Course.

That in the 1800's, harness racing was held on 3rd Avenue?

That in 1821, wealthy New Yorkers formed a jockey club and built the Union Course in Jamaica, Queens? For the next 25 years, New York City was the national center of the sport.

JAI ALAI

The urge to gamble is so universal and its practice so pleasurable that I assume it must be evil. —HEYWOOD HALE BROUN, journalist and novelist

THE STORY OF JAI ALAI BEGINS IN NORTHERN SPAIN IN THE 1600'S with a young Basque boy who injured his wrist during a handball game. Since he wanted to continue playing, he strapped on a flower basket and to everyone's surprise, retrieved and returned shots with great control and terrific speed. A new sport was born. The game ultimately moved from Spain to Cuba and then to the United States. Jai alai is very exciting and takes extraordinary agility, coordination, and skill. It's the fastest game on the planet and is more than a little dangerous. Its popularity here, however, has more to do with gambling than with the excitement of the sport.

You can pick up the game rules and different betting strategies by watching closely or buying a program, but the key words to remember are *fronton* (the playing arena), *palata* (the ball), *cesta* (the curved wicker basket used to catch and throw the ball), *cancra* (the court), and "I'VE WON!"

Milford Jai Alai (800-243-9660)
Milford, CT: Route 1-95, Exit 40
(a little over an hour's drive away)
This is the only jai alai in the area. They offer Saturday evening dinner packages, group parties with reserved seating, and weekend packages in conjunction with local hotels.

3

SPORTS that are QUIET and CALM

(BUT CAN DRIVE YOU BATTY ANYWAY)

BOWLING

One of the advantages of bowling over golf is that you seldom lose a bowling ball. —DON CARTER, champion bowler

IT'S ESTIMATED THAT 75 MILLION AMERICANS BOWL, making it the number one participation sport in the United States. And although people still play duck pins, candle pins, and barrel pins in other parts of the country, the choices here are less esoteric. It's either ten pins, ten pins, or ten pins.

It's funny, but bowling never made an impact in New York the way it did in so many other parts of the country. Maybe it's because of the mysterious scoring, the need to rent shoes, that damned heavy 16-pound ball, or the fact that "strike" is really a baseball word. But whatever the reason, there are only three places to bowl in the city itself.

Playing and Watching

Bowlmor (212-255-8188)
110 University Place, between 12th and 13th Streets
Takes up two floors of a building in Greenwich Village, and maybe all you have to know is that this is where Richard Nixon rolled a few lines and Cher threw herself a birthday party. The place has been renovated since then. There's now an expanded bar and restaurant, a renovated off-the-street lobby and elevator, and decor that can only be called 60's futuristic/psychedelic/industrial. College kids, regular folks, and colorful Village characters come here to enjoy the 44 lanes with overhead video monitors and automatic scoring.. On Monday nights, they turn off the overhead lights, crank out the glow-in-the-dark pins, and bowl and roll from 10 PM to 4 AM while a DJ spins trip, techno, house, jungle, R&B, and all-time favorites.

Corporate Sports (212-245-4738) sponsors a league at Bowlmor, which begins in September and runs through May. There are playoffs and a championship game, and both team and individual trophies are awarded. Only teams can join this league. The league is split into divisions consisting of five to ten teams of similar strength.

Chelsea Piers Bowl (212-835-2695)
West 23rd Street at the West Side Hwy
Built by AMF for $6.8 million as a showcase for its equipment and for the sport, this is about as spiffy as a bowling alley gets. It's also the first new bowling center to open in New York City in over 30 years. It features 40 lanes, automatic scoring, open play, and a whole gaggle of leagues, as well as a pro shop and video arcade—plus a cafe on the first level and a bar on the second. It also has late-night bowling to rock music with laser lights, smoke machines, Day-Glo balls, and glow-in-the-dark carpeting. It's open late every night, and round the clock on Thursday, Friday, and Saturday. I especially like the automatic ball-sizer contraption. They call it the AMF Smartball; after you stick your fingers into

this thing, an attendant will hand you a ball with the grip and weight that's right for you.

Leisure Time (212-268-6909) 625 8th Avenue on the second floor of the Port Authority Bus Terminal (entrance on the 9th Avenue side).

Features 30 modern lanes with automatic scoring and is open seven days a week. There's a pro shop, video lounge, and a sports bar and cafe. While bowling at Leisure Time you might feel as though you've stepped into an episode of *Twilight Zone.* After all, you're in a bus terminal of all places, and while most people are frantically coming or going, others never seem to leave.

Did you know?

That the automatic pinspotter was invented by Fred Schmidt of Pearl River, New York?

CRICKET

Cricket, a game which the English, not being a spiritual people, have invented in order to give themselves some conception of eternity.

—LORD MANCROFT, English politician.

CRICKET WAS PROBABLY DEVELOPED IN ENGLAND SOMETIME BEFORE THE 1400'S and is completely unfathomable to all but the initiated. It's a game with wickets, bails, stumps, bowlers, square-legs, fieldsmen, mid-offs, and popping creases. Apparently one guy throws a ball, another guy hits it and runs are scored. A game can last several days. Native New Yorkers are just too impatient to get into cricket, but since one of our glories is the number of *non*-natives who flourish here, the game is flourishing as well. There are eight different competitive leagues in the tri-state area. Three worth trying are:

Commonwealth Cricket League (Leslie Lowe at 718-601-6704)

This is the largest cricket league in the country with some 112 teams in the five boroughs. The teams are centered mostly in Brooklyn, Queens, and the Bronx, and many matches are played on one of the 14 cricket pitches in Van Cortlandt Park in the Bronx (Broadway and 252nd Street). This league is not for beginners.

Eastern American Cricket Association http://users.aol.com/eacahome/eacahome.htm

In existence since 1977, the Association is always on the prowl for talented new players. The 14 teams play their matches on Randall's Island, Staten Island, Long Island, and in Queens.

Metropolitan Cricket League (Hugh Pitter at 718-434-2739)

This league was founded in 1879, is affiliated with the International Cricket Conference, and has 21 teams in two divisions (divided by ability level). There are teams in upstate New York, New Jersey, Long Island, and Philadelphia—as well as one in Queens, six in Brooklyn, and one in the Bronx. Although many of the teams are organized around a specific country of origin, there are also a number of "mixed" teams. The season runs from the first week of May through late September.

> **Did you know?**
>
> **That the first cricket match played in this country was in 1751, and saw a team from New York City defeat a team of Londoners by a score of 166 to 130?**
>
> **That the U.S. international cricket debut took place in 1840 in Toronto? A group of underdog New Yorkers edged a strong local team by a single run.**

CROQUET

It is no game for the soft of sinew and the gentle of spirit. The higher and dirtier croquet player can use the guile of a cobra and the inhumanity of a boa constrictor. —ALEXANDER WOLLCOTT, writer and critic

OH, I GUESS THERE'S STILL SOME CACHET ATTACHED TO PLAYING CROQUET on a lush Connecticut lawn with a remote descendent of the Great Gatsby, but playing in Central Park, now *there's* an attention getter at any cocktail party.

Playing and Watching

The New York Croquet Club (212-369-7949)
Bowling green north of Sheep Meadow, mid-Central Park at about 69th Street

The largest croquet organization in the United States, this club has over 150 members, some of whom are among the top players in the country. The season runs from early May to early November and features numerous tournaments. Members can also use the facility for individual practice and play. The club is private, and annual dues include the city permit you need to use the green. Teaching clinics are offered at 6 PM every Tuesday from the middle of May to late September. Wear white apparel and flat-soled shoes or sneakers. And by the way, competition-level croquet is different from the backyard game your suburban friends nagged you into playing at their last barbecue. The court is larger, the wickets are narrower, the mallets are heavier, and there are differences in the strokes and strategies.

Did you know?
That the first American croquet club was founded in Brooklyn, in 1862? It was called the Park Place Croquet Club and had 25 members.

CURLING

THIS MAY BE ONE OF THOSE SPORTS YOU'VE ONLY SEEN ON *THE WIDE WORLD OF SPORTS.* In curling, a player uses a twist of the wrist to slide a polished granite stone down a track of ice while teammates with brooms furiously sweep its path clean. People have been playing this sport since the middle 1500's, and if *you're* interested you can call Victor Heubner to get the scoop on curling in the metro area (office: 212-468-0540, home: 914-693-4741).

Victor will tell you about the Ardsley Curling Club in Westchester, which is about a half hour away by car or the Metro North. The club was founded in 1932 and has three enclosed playing-areas (called *sheets*). The season runs from late October to the end of March. They always have an open house in October so you can tour the facility, observe the sport, and get some free training. The club has men's, women's, and coed curling; sends teams to competitions in the United States, Canada, and Europe; and hosts national and international *bonspiels* (tournaments)—usually in late February. And when you talk to Victor, ask him about the New York Caledonian Curling Club. This club is said to be the oldest sporting club in the country and actually used a pond in Central Park as its first curling site.

GOLF

Golf is a game whose aim is to hit a very small ball into an even smaller hole, with weapons singularly ill-designed for the purpose.
—WINSTON CHURCHILL, English statesman

EW YORK HAS 13 PUBLIC GOLF COURSES LOCATED IN EVERY BOROUGH EXCEPT MANHATTAN, each with its own character. Although none are as lush or expansive as their private counterparts, the prices are hard to beat. You can play on any of these courses with and without a permit, which, if you play regularly, is a real money-saver (available at any course for $6 and proof that you live here). And for only $2 you can make a reservation at most of the city courses by calling 718-225-4653.

Playing

THE BRONX

Van Cortlandt Park Golf Course (718-543-4595)
Van Cortlandt Park South and Bailey Avenue

This is the oldest 18-hole public course in the country, featuring plenty of trees and two water hazards. The narrow course is a par 70, 5913-yarder, appropriate for players of all skill levels, and its signature hole is #2 (a 620-yard par 5). If you're a twosome, you can call ahead to reserve. Instruction is available, as well as food and a pro shop. The course can be reached by subway, but be forewarned you will pass through a few rough neighborhoods.

Mosholu Golf Course (718-655-9164)
3700 Jerome Avenue

A nine-hole, 3,263-yarder that most golfers play through twice. Tee markers make it a par 35 for the first nine, and par 36 for the second. This course is not in the best shape and attracts a high percentage of beginning golfers. Instruction is available, as is a lighted driving range with 46 mats and 29 grass tees.

Split Rock Golf Course & Pelham Golf Course (718-885-1258)
870 North Shore Road, Pelham

The Par 72, 6,281-yard Split Rock and the par 71, 6,405-yard Pelham sit side-by-side in the Northwest Bronx. Pelham has wide fairways and gentle slopes, while Split Rock has narrow fairways, lots of trees, and is the tougher of the two. In fact, it was rated as the city's "most challenging" course in a *New York* magazine survey.

BROOKLYN

Dyker Beach Golf Course (718-836-9722)
86th Street and Seventh Avenue, Dyker Heights

Designed by John Van Kleek, this scenic, 6,736 yard tree-lined course has no water hazards and the terrain is generally flat, wide, and straightaway. Considered challenging by many, Dyker generally draws capable players. Instruction is

available, and the course is easily accessible by subway (R line).

Marine Park Golf Course (718-338-7149)
2800 Flatbush, Marine Park

Located near Rockaway Bay, Marine Park is a long and windy 6,609-yard par 72 with a flat and wide course that draws big crowds. For practice there are three putting greens, and instruction is also available.

QUEENS

Clearview Golf Course (718-229-2570)
202-12 Willets Point Boulevard, Bayside

This is a mostly flat, mostly straight, 6,283-yard par 70 with an attractive view of Long Island Sound. It is well-maintained, with wide, tree-lined fairways, and small and challenging greens. It's best for beginner to intermediate players, and can get crowded on weekends. Instruction is available, and there is a pro shop and food. Unfortunately, the course is difficult to reach without a car.

Douglaston Golf Course (718-428-1617)
6320 Marathon Parkway, Douglaston

A 5,140-yard par 67 with lots of hills and a few water hazards that's said to be the most-played course in the city. Instruction is available. You *really* need a car to get there.

Forest Park Golf Course (718-296-0999)
101 Forest Park Drive, Woodhaven

A moderately difficult 5,920-yard par 69, with narrow fairways, hills, lots of trees, and three water hazards. The course was refurbished in 1997 and has authentic small town charm. There's a clubhouse and instruction. You'll need a car to get there.

STATEN ISLAND

La Tourette Golf Course (718-351-1889)
1001 Richmond Hill Road, Richmondtown

Set on 422 acres of wooded parkland, some say this 6,322-yard par 72 is the #1 course in the city because of its layout, variety of holes, and perfect condition. The course has four water hazards and a back nine with lots of hills. It's for all skill levels, yet even advanced golfers admit it's a challenge. La Tourette also has a driving range, a putting green overlooking the course, and a clubhouse that was built in 1836. There is a pro shop and food, and instruction is available from an on-site PGA teaching pro. The course is about a 20-minute/$10 cab ride from the Staten Island Ferry.

Silver Lake Golf Course (718-447-5686)
915 Victory Boulevard, Stapleton

Situated in a 107-acre city park with views of Manhattan and New Jersey's Watchung Mountains, this is a challenging 5,736-yard par 69 with tight fairways, three water hazards, a hilly front nine, level back nine, and plenty of trees. There is a putting green, pro shop, and food—but no instruction. Although the course isn't long, it's challenging due to its hills and its elevated tees and greens. It's not overly crowded, and since Staten Island is still relatively bucolic in places, the people there have a little less *edge* than you're likely to find elsewhere. The course is about a five-minute bus or cab ride from the ferry.

FURTHER AWAY

Bethpage State Park
(516-249-0707)
Farmingdale, Long Island
(about 1-1/2 hours away)

This is the home of Bethpage Black, regularly ranked among the top 25 public courses in the country, and the site of the 2002 U.S. Open. In terms of location, this is unquestionably the closest, world-class *public* course where a New Yorker can play. It's very long, and its length is matched by the amount and density of rough. To enjoy playing here, you better be good—or you better have a healthy sense of humor about your game. Come to think of it, if you have a healthy sense of humor about your game, you probably don't play at all.

Concord Hotel
(914-794-4000)
Kiamesha Lake, NY (about 90 miles away)

"The Monster" is consistently voted by *Golf Digest* as one of the top 100 public courses in the country.

James Baird State Park
(914-473-1052)
Pleasant Valley, NY (about 75 miles away)

A well-maintained course designed by Robert Trent Jones.

Spook Rock
(914-357-6466)
Ramapo, NY (about 50 miles away)

Golf Digest gives Spook Rock consistently high ratings.

Can't Sleep Before You Play the Third Hole at Augusta?

Then **Heartland Golf Park (516-667-7400)** in Brentwood, Long Island (across from the LIRR Deer Park station) is for you because the last tee time is 3 AM. This is a nine-hole, par 3 course that replicates famous holes from some of the great courses in the world. There is also miniature golf (open to 3 AM as well) and a 24-hour driving range. Heartland gives entirely new meaning to the term "golf widow."

Driving Ranges

Chelsea Piers
(212-336-6400)
West 23rd Street at the West Side Hwy

An absolutely amazing setting for driving golf balls, this range is four-tiers high, with 52 heated cages, automatic ball replacement, and a 200-yard fairway. It seems as though you're actually hitting balls right into the Hudson River. The range opens early and doesn't close until late, and there's a pro shop, club rentals, a 1000-square foot putting green, and a clubhouse. A golf academy located on-site offers clinics and private, semiprivate, and group lessons to help you improve your swing, putting, bunker shots, pitching, and chipping. The academy uses stop motion video and swing analysis computers, and offers a wide variety of membership packages.

Golden Bear Alley Pond Park
(718-225-9187)
Northern Boulevard at 231st Street, Queens

Features 80 tees lit for night play, a putting green, and a chipping area with sand trap. Instruction is available and there is also a pro shop and two 18-hole miniature golf courses, which are lit for night play as well.

Randall's Island Family Golf Center (212-427-5689)

The Family Golf Center has a driving range with 106 tees and offers instruction from a PGA teaching pro. (For more information about Randall's Island, see page 16.)

Turtle Cove Golf Complex (718-885-2646)
1 City Island Road, City Island

The complex has 120 tees and a 300-yard fairway, plus lessons from a PGA teaching pro. And why not try your hand at their 18-hole miniature golf course? (For more information about City Island itself, including where to enjoy some great seafood, see page 16).

And if You Feel Like Pitching and Putting

A Pitch and Putt course is simply a regular golf course on a much smaller scale. The distance between holes is shorter, every hole is a par three, and you are required to negotiate the whole thing (while keeping your sanity) with just two clubs: a wedge and a putter. Four of the closest options are: **Breezy Point (718-474-1623),** Jacob Riis Park, Queens, open mid-March through November; **Flushing Meadows (718-271-8182),** Corona Park, Queens, open year-round; **Robert Moses State Park (516-669-0470),** Babylon, Long Island, open April through November; and **Lincoln Park Golf Course (201-332-2100),** Jersey City (PATH Train and then a five-minute cab ride), open year-round.

Learning and Buying

Richard Metz Golf Studio (212-759-6940)
425 Madison Avenue at 49th Street

A retail store and instruction facility, over 8,000 lessons annually are given to players of all levels by three, full-time PGA pros. The instructors use video and computer swing analysis to help improve your game (or give you the beginnings of one if you're just starting out). Lessons can be purchased in blocks of ten half-hours, and you have a year to use them up.

5th Avenue Golf Center (754-9398)
581 Fifth Avenue between 47th and 48th Streets

A retail shop and teaching facility with a putting green and a teaching room where you hit into a net. Each lesson is videotaped, and if you bring your own tape you can study your stroke at home and weep in private. Half-hour lessons are available in blocks of four.

Outings

The NYC Golf Club (718-792-1378) makes arrangements for Manhattanites at over 20 different courses within shouting distance of town. Daily outings are offered. Transportation is provided in a customized van large enough for three foursomes and gear. The club has a membership fee—plus individual transportation costs and greens fees. They also run a golf school, so ask for details when you call.

Golf Simulators

New York Health & Racquet Indoor Golf and Country Club (212-422-4653)
39 Whitehall Street, between Pearl and Water Streets

Two state-of-the-art golf simulators are free for club members and available for a fee to nonmembers. After you take a real club and swing at a full-size video screen, sensors take over, measuring the trajectory of your shot and its exact distance. The simulator shows hooks and slices, plays hazards, and keeps score. You can even choose to play one of eight different courses (like Augusta and Pebble Beach). In addition to the simulators, this facility has a putting green, a computerized swing analyzer, clinics, individual and group lessons with a PGA teaching pro, free use of equipment, a pro shop, and lockers.

College Golf:

Columbia University (Manhattan) 212-854-2546

Long Island University (Brooklyn) 718-488-1240

St. John's University (Queens) 718-990-6367

Did you know?

That a form of miniature golf was played in New York City in 1652? A small ball was putted around a green with a crooked club.

LAWN BOWLING

EVER SEE LAWN BOWLING IN CENTRAL PARK? The players look like they're from an exclusive *someplace else,* and the game from a *genteel time* long ago. Well, the players are actually real people, the bowling green is a public facility, free lessons are available—and all you need to get involved is white clothing and flat shoes.

The New York Lawn Bowling Club and the Metropolitan Lawn Bowling Club of New York share the green. Either club can help you with equipment and lessons, and arrange for the city permit you need to use the green. For information on **The Metropolitan Lawn Bowling Club of New York** call Richard Keoseian (212-799-5151), and for the lowdown on **The New York Lawn Bowling Club** call Jane Jacobs (212-877-9890) or Dong Kingman (212-345-5573).

The bowling green is north of Sheep Meadow, mid-park at about 69th Street. The season runs from May to November and includes about ten Saturday tournaments. Aside from Saturday and Monday, there's regular play every other day of the week.

Did you know?

That the Dutch brought lawn bowling here in 1626, and that Bowling Green (at the southern tip of Manhattan) was North America's first official park?

That in order to establish the green, "a piece of land at the lower end of broadway fronting the fort" was leased in 1732 to three well-known New Yorkers for the price of one peppercorn?

That George Washington bowled there?

POOL AND BILLIARDS

Dressing a pool player in a tuxedo is like putting whipped cream on a hot dog.

—MINNESOTA FATS, professional pool player (and hustler)

IT USED TO BE THAT POOL HALLS FELL INTO TWO CATEGORIES: new, clean and trendy; or old, grungy and atmospheric. And the place you chose to play typically depended on the images that shooting pool conjured in your mind—images probably from Paul Newman movies like *The Hustler* and *The Color of Money.*

You can still go to the new, clean, trendy places where you put down your briefcase, take off your suit jacket, and drink a $5 Corona with a piece of lime stuck in it. But, nowadays there are far fewer places with cigarette burns on the tables, "No Gambling or Swearing" signs on the walls, and the ghost of Fast Eddie racking them up at the next table.

And speaking of Fast Eddie, you still have to be careful about the guy who sidles up and asks if you'd like to play a "friendly little game." Say yes, and his beat-up old house cue will be replaced by the custom job that was resting in its velvet-lined case, patiently waiting for little old you.

Playing and Watching and Learning

Amsterdam Billiards Club (212-496-8180) 344 Amsterdam Avenue between 76th and 77th Streets

Offers 30 tables, food, cues for sale, and occasional appearances by comedian David Brenner, who co-owns the place. Amsterdam is so clean and well-kept you could bring your mother. They have an 8-ball league, a 9-ball league (for intermediate and advanced players only), and clinics for beginners and intermediates. The beginners learn stance, basic strokes, bridges, strategy, and carom shots. Intermediates practice stroke techniques, position play, and game strategies. There is also an East Side Amsterdam (212-570-4545) at 210 East 86th, between 2nd and 3rd Avenues. You have to walk past a wall of pool champions to get to the front desk, and, if you look at the pictures closely enough, you'll see David "Sticks" Brenner right up there with the all-time greats.

The Billiard Club (212-206-7665) 220 West 19th Street between 7th and 8th Avenues

Takes up two floors of a converted warehouse with 33 tables, brass chandeliers, and a snack bar.

Chelsea Billiards (212-989-0096) 54 West 21st Street between 5th and 6th Avenues

A very spacious loft-like setting with 40 pool, eight snooker, and two billiards tables. This is a real pool hall during the week, but more of a couples/singles hangout on weekend evenings. Chelsea hosts corporate events, offers instruction, sponsors tournaments, and has a pro shop and snack bar.

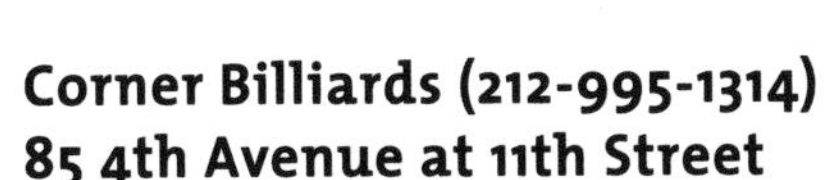

Corner Billiards (212-995-1314)
85 4th Avenue at 11th Street
Named the "best pool hall in New York" by a *New York* magazine survey. There are 28 tables, plus a full "gourmet" cafe and a strong selection of microbrews. Corner has leagues for 9-ball, 8-ball, and straight pool. Each runs about ten weeks, plus playoffs and championship games. In addition, the American Billiard School is in operation here, with beginning through advanced instruction for both individuals and groups.

Eastside Billiards Club (212-831-7665)
163 East 86th Street between Lexington and Third Avenues
At the top of two long flights of stairs, which makes it feel like you're going to a real old-time pool hall, you'll find 18 well-lit Brunswick Gold Crown tables. This club offers leagues, tournaments, ladies nights, instruction, beer, food, couches, video games, and satellite TV. This is a very comfortable place, which feels as much like a billiards lounge as a pool hall. Eastside stays open very late every night of the week.

Le Q (212-995-8512)
36 East 12th Street between University Place and Broadway
This pool hall is open 24 hours a day and, due to its location, is very popular with NYU students. There are 27 pool tables on two floors, with one billiards table on the first floor and two Ping Pong tables downstairs. As an added bonus, they have an eclectic jukebox that mixes rap with heavy metal and oldies.

Tournaments

The Mayor's Cup Billiards Tournament, open to men and women, is held every spring (in April or May). The preliminary rounds take place in 16 pool halls (at least one in every borough) and the playoffs and final match are typically held in Manhattan. For entry information, schedules, and locations, call the New York City Sports Commission (212-788-8389).

Surfing the Net

Billiard Congress of America
http://www.bca-pool.com/
Find news, products, tournaments, publications, leagues, and links to other sites. Pretty high-tech for a bunch of guys whose mothers were afraid they were wasting their youth.

Did you know?:
That Julian's Famous Poolroom, the oldest pool hall in New York, and the film set for scenes from *The Hustler*, was closed in 1997 after 68 years? The site may already have been converted into NYU dorms where, no doubt, the ghost of Minnesota Fats is inhabiting all the best rooms, and the faint clack of ivory balls can be heard whispering down the halls. Rest in Peace.

4
SPORTS
played with
SHARP
or
DANGEROUS
THINGS

ARCHERY

America's first archery club, The United Bowmen, was founded in Philadelphia in 1828 by a group of artists. Membership required a $5 initiation fee, monthly dues of 50 cents, and the most splendid uniform: a green Lincoln frock coat with gold trim, and a straw hat decorated with three ostrich plumes. There is no record of how well the Bowmen could shoot—but nobody ever looked better.

Shooting and Watching and Learning

INDOOR RANGES

Olinville Arms (718-655-1569)
33-56 White Plains Road between Gunhill Road and Burke Avenue, Bronx

A 20-yard range that can accommodate ten archers shooting at regular and animal targets. No rental equipment is available, but you can get instruction by calling ahead. Olinville is open to the general public and accessible by subway and bus.

Proline Archery Range
(718-845-9280)
95-11 101 Avenue between Woodhaven Blvd and 95th, Ozone Park, Queens

Has 30 positions and a 20-yard range with paper targets. Rental equipment and instruction are available, along with a snack bar and a fully-stocked pro shop. The range runs year-round coed target and hunting leagues.

Pro-Stop Archery Range
(718-232-4040)
7923 New Utrecht Avenue between 78th and 80th Streets, Brooklyn

Offers 12 lanes and a 20-yard range. Shoot at paper targets or try your hand at the laserdisc simulations that portray virtual animals in the wild, complete with sound effects. Rental equipment is available, as is instruction. Pro-Stop runs men's, women's, and coed leagues—and is accessible by subway and bus.

Queens Archery
(718-461-1756)
170-20 39th Avenue, at 171st Street, Flushing, Queens

In business for over 30 years, Queens has 20 lanes 20 yards long where you can shoot at targets or, with the aid of a slide projection system at pictures of game animals in natural settings. This is not a club, so you don't have to work around blocks of time already reserved by one organization or another. There are four target and hunting leagues (including a coed league), and rental equipment is available. A free lesson is offered, courtesy of the owner, who claims one lesson is all that it takes, and then it's practice, practice, practice. The range is accessible by bus, subway, and the Long Island Railroad.

College Archery

Columbia University (women's team)
212-854-2546

Did you know? That there is a sport called Archery Golf? It's played on a specially prepared course that uses flight arrows for "driving" and field arrows for "putting." There is a stroke for each arrow shot, and you hole out by hitting a special target. The game is based on a form of competition dating from the 16th century called *roving*. Archers would set up a course, mark various locations, and the marksman who used the fewest arrows to complete the course was declared the winner.

DARTS

DARTS WAS PLAYED IN THE MIDDLE AGES TO TRAIN ENGLISH ARCHERS, and heavily-weighted darts (actually "throwing arrows") were used for self-defense in Ireland during the 1500's. Our very own Pilgrims played darts aboard the *Mayflower,* and the game grew from there to became popular in pubs and inns in the 19th and 20th centuries.

To get involved with this sport, go to one of the genuine dart bars around town. All these places have teams that play in a regular Monday and Tuesday night league. This isn't a have-a-beer-and-giggle league: Each night 400 competitors from women's and men's teams play. There are captains and divisions and sub-divisions, and rules, regulations, and a governing body—the New York Darts Organization. There are also numerous tournaments throughout the year, and each bar posts announcements of upcoming events on their bulletin board.

Playing and Watching and Learning

Bleecker Street Bar (212-334-0244)
59 Bleecker Street between Lafayette and Broadway

The Edge (212-477-2940)
95 East 3rd Street between 1st and 2nd Avenues

Garden Tavern (212-643-1502)
407 8th Avenue between 30th and 31st Streets

Kettle of Fish (212-533-4790)
130 West 3rd Street between 6th Avenue and McDougal Street

McAleers (212-874-8037)
425 Amsterdam Avenue between 81st and 82nd Streets

Pour House (212-987-3790)
1712 2nd Avenue at 89th Street

Sandy's Place (212-599-9349)
699 2nd Avenue between 37th and 38th Streets

Equipment

All Fun and Games (212-366-6981)
160 West 26th Street between 6th and 7th Avenues

Sells standard and custom darts in all price ranges ($5 to over $150).

The Dart Shoppe (212-533-8684)
30 East 20th Street between Broadway and Park Avenue

Sells everything for darts—and only for darts. Talk to Jim Birmingham, and he will give you a free lesson.

Surfing the Net

The American Darts Organization's *Dartlines*
http://www.infohwy.com:80/darts/

Offers information on the basics and rules of the game, as well as tournament schedules, feature stories, a chat room, and more.

FENCING

Pay your respects to the Gods and Buddhas, but never rely on them.

—MIYAMOTO MUSASHI, 17th-century Japanese swordsman

SO WHO KNEW? Not only can you fence in New York, but you can fence four different ways: sport (like in the Olympics), classical (like in the 17th and 18th centuries), theatrical (like in the movies), and Japanese (like in *Shogun*).

Sport

Blade Fencing (212-620-0114)
212 West 15th Street between 7th and 8th Avenues

Offers private, ten-lesson packages in foil, saber, and epee for fencers at all levels. Loaner equipment is available.

McBurney YMCA (212-741-9210)
215 West 23rd Street between 7th and 8th Avenues

Offers three-hour classes in group fencing two evenings a week. Private instruction is available in sets of six lessons.

Metropolis Fencing School (212-463-8044) 45 West 21st Street between 5th and 6th Avenues, on the 2nd floor
Conducts group lessons in foil, advanced foil, sabre, and epee. The price of the lessons includes use of equipment. The staff of instructors reads like a fencing *Who's Who*, with an impressive mix of U.S. and international champions, coaches, and Olympians. Metropolitan has seven fencing strips, is open daily, and also functions as a club (yearly memberships are available).

The New York Fencers Club (212-874-9800) 154 West 71st Street between Broadway and Columbus Avenue
This is the oldest fencing club in the country. You can choose from among many different membership packages, depending on your age, skill level, and appetite for lessons and practice. NOTE: The club will be relocating in the near future.

Riverbank State Park (212-694-3600) Hudson River at 145th Street
Beginning fencing classes on Saturday afternoons.

Historical

Martinez Classical Fencing (201-330-8670) Studio KHDT, 330 Broome Street (a half-block east of Bowery)
An academy that, to quote its brochure: "preserves the tradition of viewing fencing as the study of sword in its realistic application in personal combat." The school offers classical fencing (19th- and early 20th-century French and Italian foil, epee, and Italian sabre) and historical swordsmanship (18th-century French and Italian smallsword, and 17th-century Spanish and Italian rapier). The classes are based on the fencing academies of the past, where students were taught individually and encouraged to develop their own style. Martinez is careful to point out that they don't teach sport or theatrical fencing, and that they practice with every weapon as if they were really going to use it.

Theatrical

You can take workshops and classes at these two acting schools even if not enrolled as a regular student.

American Academy of Dramatic Arts (212-686-9244) 120 Madison Avenue between 30th and 31st Streets
Offers an evening workshop that runs for six weeks.

HB Studio (212-675-2370) 120 Bank Street between Greenwich and Washington Streets
Offers fencing classes at various levels.

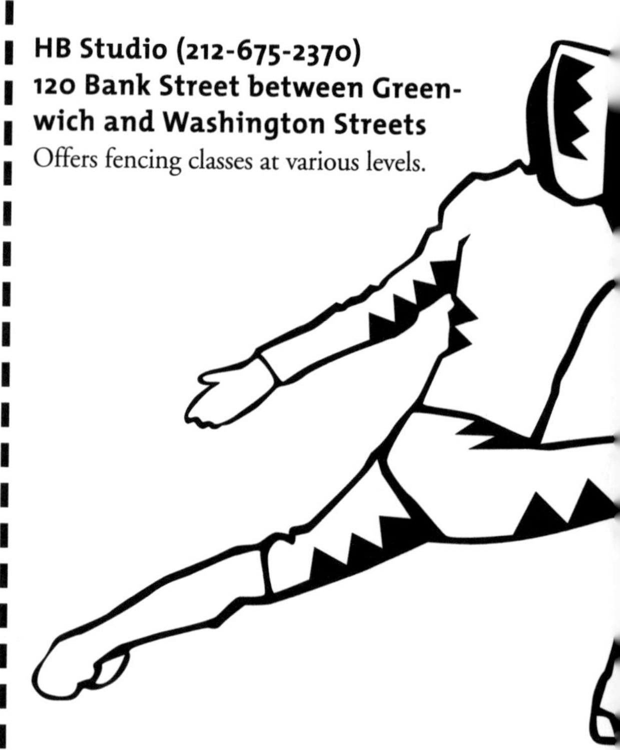

Japanese

The Japanese Swordsmanship Society (212-691-2891)

Classes are held in the foremost weapon of the Samurai—the *Nipponto.* This sword is used to deliver a counterattack in the martial art Iaido. There is no sport or competitive aspect to Iaido, and its techniques are taught by practicing *katas,* (prearranged solo exercises that must be done with great precision). Classes in Iaido are offered Tuesday evenings and Saturday and Sunday mornings at two downtown locations. Call to get on the mailing list.

College Fencing

Columbia University (Manhattan)
212-854-2546

New York University (Manhattan)
212-998-2029

St. John's University (Queens)
718-990-6367

Surfing the Net

The United States Fencing Association http://www.usfa.org/

Provides information on clubs, scheduled events, the U.S. National and Olympic Teams, rules and regulations, and point standings for various age categories. There are also multiple links to other fencing sites.

Did you know?

That the first national fencing championships were held in New York City at the Berkeley Lyceum?

HOCKEY

Now I can finally die in peace.
—A FAN'S T-SHIRT, after the New York Rangers captured the Stanley Cup in 1994 for the first time in 54 years.

Playing

Chelsea Piers Sky Rink (212-336-6100)
West 23rd Street at the West Side Hwy

Sky Rink has a regulation NHL-size rink and a popular hockey league, with teams in five divisions which each play a 12-game schedule, plus playoffs. For players with limited or no experience, there's an instructional league. The Sky Rink offers clinics on basic skating and puck control. There is open hockey every day (including a pickup game at noon), and a regular Friday late-night (12:30–2:30 AM) game. Call ahead to reserve a spot.

Hockey North America (800-4-HOCKEY) is the largest adult ice hockey league in North America. About 600 men and women play on 30 to 35 intermediate and eight beginner teams. It's all non-checking, and you can start with eight weeks of beginner training and then move into eight weeks of league play. If you already know your way around the game, you can start in an intermediate league. The games are played at various sites around the area, with Westchester currently being the closest.

Lasker Rink (212-534-7639)
Mid-Central Park at 106th Street

A hockey league and pickup games start at the beginning of November and run through the end of March. Call for schedules and league information. This, by the way, is a picturesque spot, surrounded by hills with wonderful old trees, overlooking the Harlem Meer lake. A series of natural pools and a small waterfall are just a short walk away.

Professional Hockey

Devils (201-935-6050)
Continental Airlines Arena,
East Rutherford, NJ
http://www.nhl.com/teams/nj/index.htm

Although good tickets are hard to come by, the arena rarely sells out, so call or visit the box office and see how lucky you can get. New Jersey Transit buses will get you there from the Port Authority (973-762-5100).

Islanders (516-794-9300)
Nassau Veterans Memorial Coliseum,
Uniondale, Long Island
http://www.nhl.com/teams/nyi/index.htm

The Islanders have had solid fan support for years, so be sure to call the box office ahead of time to check for ticket availability. Since there is no direct public transportation to the Coliseum, taking in an Islanders game necessitates renting a car, another reason to make certain

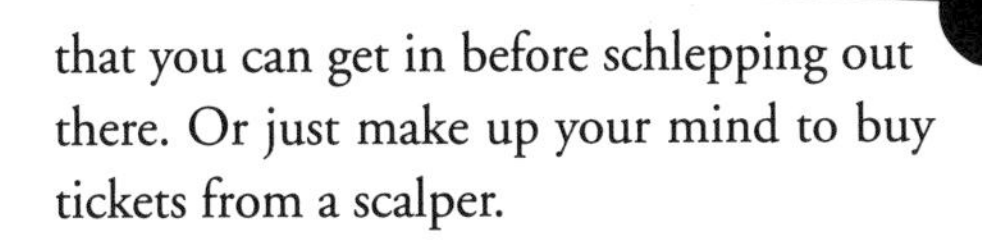

that you can get in before schlepping out there. Or just make up your mind to buy tickets from a scalper.

Rangers (212-465-6741)
Madison Square Garden, 7th Avenue, between 31st and 33rd Streets
http://www.newyorkrangers.com/
Tickets? Very hard to come by, so get invited, watch them on TV, or try a scalper.

Roller and In-line Hockey

Chelsea Piers (212-336-6200)
West 23rd Street at the West Side Hwy
There are two open-air, concrete roller rinks and a very active league with three divisions and 12-game schedules, plus playoffs. In addition, Chelsea Piers offers clinics, four-on-four tournaments, and pickup games. In fact, you can get into a pickup game at lunchtime, from noon-2 PM, on Monday, Wednesday, and Friday.

Robert Moses Playground
41st Street and 1st Avenue
The best roller hockey rink in the city and a good bet for weekend pickup games.

Carl Shurz Park
East 84th Street and East End Avenue
This roller hockey rink is directly adjacent to three half-court basketball courts, so play nice, boys.

The Pros

Rockin' Rollers (201-507-1303)
Continental Arena, East Rutherford, NJ
The Rollers play in the Roller Hockey International League, which was formed in 1992 and, as with many new leagues, has had its ups and downs. Some franchises have flourished, while others have gone belly-up. Happily, the Rockin' Rollers have enjoyed strong fan support from the get-go. The league plays a summer season with playoffs, division championships, and a late August world championship. Call for a schedule.

Did you know?
That Brooklyn once had a National Hockey League franchise? The team began as the New York Americans but folded during World War II. Just before this happened, however, they changed their name to the *Brooklyn* Americans.

ICE SKATING

Skating and Watching and Learning

Chelsea Piers Sky Rink (212-336-6100)
West 23rd Street at the West Side Hwy

Two indoor ice rinks, one of which is Olympic-size and usually reserved for general, figure, and speed skating. There is a full pro shop, a pizza snack bar, and skate rentals. There's also private, semiprivate, and group instruction at all levels—plus a special beginners class. If you really get good (or are already) you can attend workshops with the Ice Theater of New York. Between its many offerings—open skating, rink rentals, lessons, and hockey—Sky Rink is open 22 hours a day, 363 days a year.

Ice Studio (212-535-0304)
1034 Lexington Avenue between 73rd and 74th Streets

On the second floor of a brownstone, this small rink offers open skating and instruction.

Lasker Rink (212-534-7639)
Mid-Central Park at 106th Street

Ice skating is available from the beginning of November through the end of March. There is open skating whenever the rink isn't being used for league hockey and pickup games. Equipment rentals and lessons are available. (For more information about Lasker Rink, see page 52).

Riverbank State Park (212-694-3600)
Hudson River at 145th Street

Here you'll find an enclosed 200' x 85' covered rink that offers ice skating in the winter (November through March) and roller skating in the summer. Beginning and intermediate instruction is available, and you can rent skates. It's the atmosphere of a neighborhood rink, with families and kids and lots of noise.

Rockefeller Center Skating Rink (212-332-7654)
49th Street and 5th Avenue

Magical at night, and especially at Christmas time, Rockefeller Center is the most romantic skating location in town. There you are on the ice, admiring the twinkling lights of the tree and surrounding buildings, gazing at the golden statue of Prometheus, and looking up at the hordes of tourists. On second thought, if you're usually on your butt more than on your skates, a less public venue might be better. Prometheus won't react, but the tourists might giggle. Lessons and rentals, from October to mid-April.

Wollman Rink (212-396-1010)
Mid-Central Park at 62nd Street

The setting is magnificent: There's something wonderful about being surrounded by grass and trees in a park, and then looking up at a skyline of fabulous buildings.

This 33,000-square foot rink's season runs from mid-October to the end of April. Equipment rentals and lessons are available.

PAINTBALL

YOU SAY YOU WANT TO GET TOGETHER WITH A GANG OF ROWDY FRIENDS, put on camouflage clothes, and run around in the woods shooting people with paint pellets? You say you enjoy playing war games, hiding behind trees and rocks, setting ambushes, and shouting and hollering? You say you enjoy the adrenaline rush, and it's OK that you're out of the game if you get hit? You say you know that the pellets contain nontoxic, noncaustic, water-soluble, biodegradable paint that's enclosed in the gelatin used to make cold capsules? And you say you know that paintball typically has .31 injuries per 1,000 participants yearly as opposed to 223.79 for lacrosse? OK, say no more.

Outdoors

New Jersey Paintball Club (973-838-7493 or 973-839-3078) Butler, New Jersey (about a 45-minute drive from Manhattan)

The club has nine playing fields on 137 acres of woods, trails, ledges, and rock formations. Morning and afternoon sessions are available, and the club offers a variety of package deals—depending on how much you want to play. They also have an ongoing schedule of special events and tournaments, including role-playing scenarios such as a reconstruction of the Battle of Gettysburg. this club considers itself a membership club and reserves the right to refuse participation to those they think are safety risks to themselves or others. Their season runs Saturdays and Sundays from mid-March to mid-December, but you can arrange to play on a weekday if you bring a large enough group. You can even reserve a private field if you bring 25 people or more.

Skirmish U.S.A. (800-SKIRMISH) Route 903, Jim Thorpe, PA (about 2 hours away in the Poconos)

The 39 playing fields here range in size from five to 50 acres: 700 acres overall, with a variety of terrain, that includes dense underbrush, open woodland, creeks, and bridges. In addition, six of the fields contain villages, towers, or forts. Skirmish is open daily year-round, and groups of 20 or more can rent a private field. They continually run tournaments and special events, so call for more information. You can combine your paintball with Class 2 and 3 whitewater rafting on the upper and lower Lehigh River Gorge. Canoeing, kayaking, hiking, camping, and mountain biking are also available.

Survival New York and Paintball Long Island (800-FLAG 007 or 914-241-0020) Plattekill, New York (near Newburgh, about 90 minutes north of the George Washington Bridge) Coram, Long Island (about 40 minutes from the Queens/Nassau border)

Both facilities are open Saturday and Sunday year-round, except during extreme weather conditions. Either will open any day of the week for a group of 20 or more. Registration is at 8:30 AM sharp, and you'll be out until at least 5 PM playing hide-and-seek, cops-and-robbers, and capture-the-flag. In addition, both facilities host numerous special events, tournaments, and trade shows. You can do a 28-hour fantasy scenario game (yes, 28 hours) and join what they call the Big Game, in which over 1,000 players do combat on over 60 acres (yes, 1,000 players, and yes, 60 acres).

Indoors

Oceanside Indoor Paintball (516-766-3636) 3415 Hampton Road, Oceanside, New York

Exactly 12,000 square feet of indoor mayhem with obstacles to run around, bunkers to hide in, and walls to climb over. They play capture-the-flag and all its variations daily, 52 weeks a year. Since the playing schedule changes seasonally, call for the latest information.

Did you know?
That the first game of paintball was played to settle an argument in New Hampshire between a city boy and a country boy? The question was who could survive the longest, using basic skills and common sense. So they recruited ten of their friends, chose teams, rounded up some color-marking guns from a forestry catalog and played capture-the-flag. Alas, the country boy won.

POLO

They met on the polo fields. But then, doesn't everyone? —SARAH FERGUSON'S MOTHER, commenting on how Fergie met Prince Andrew

Playing and Learning and Watching

Blue Sky Polo Club (914-692-2922) Middletown, NY (about 65 miles north of town)

Blue Sky has two stick and ball fields, one practice field, and one Sunday field—all set on a 400-acre farm with a clubhouse and plenty of room for boarding. Their season typically runs from May through the end of September, with practices and matches three or four days a week and monthly tournaments. Argentine and American pros are available for lessons and play, and there are various fee schedules—depending on what services you're interested in.

Chelsea Equestrian Center (212-376-9090) West 23rd Street and the Hudson River

This facility doesn't have a large enough ring for full-out matches, but call to see if they're hosting any informal pickup games or practice sessions.

Gardnertown Polo Club
(914-564-6658)
Newburgh, NY (about 1-1/2 hours away)

Founded in 1990, they only play indoors here, from October through April, in their 200' x 100' arena. Tournaments are held frequently, usually on Friday evenings. The club offers horses for lease at seasonal rates as well as boarding. Group and private lessons are by appointment.

Meadowbrook Polo Club
(516-681-5300)
Old Westbury, Long Island
(about 45 minutes away from the city)

Meadowbrook is the successor to the famed club of the same name that existed in the 20's and 30's, and stood at the forefront of polo in this country. In fact, Meadowbrook holds the longest continuous registration within the United States Polo Association, dating back to 1881. The club is a frequent host of the U.S. Open, and has a total of five fields and stabling for over 200 horses. Their main tournament field is in Bethpage State Park, and it is fully equipped with an electronic scoreboard and seating for 500. The other fields are located in Old Westbury. The club has about 50 members, and its season runs from May to October. Members play on weekends and two weekday evenings.

Southampton Polo Club
(call Frank McNamara at 212-681-2828)
Southampton, Long Island

Southampton is the largest club on Long Island, with about 26 participating members and ten or so pros who play with them. Games are played at a beginner to intermediate level. Those who want to learn the sport are welcome, but if you're a beginner, it's best to start on a borrowed horse and then lease or buy after you're hooked.

Riding the Net

The United States Polo Association
http://www.uspolo.org/

Information about events, players, clubs, rules, and links to other sites.

Bike Polo

As the name suggests, this is polo without a horse, which doesn't require the bucks needed to maintain one. It's thought that the game began in India about 100 years ago when British troops used bicycles to help improve their regular polo skills. In the 70's and early 80's, New York was the center of bike polo in this country, but currently the game is no longer played here. If it rankles you that there's a sport in which New Yorkers don't participate, don't just sit there. Get some friends together. All you need is a bike, a helmet, a mallet, and a ball—and then make up some rules. How hard could it be?

If you're a stickler for the real thing, you can get in touch with the **Bicycle Polo Association** (916-979-9800, fax: 916-979-9900), 3638 American River Drive, Suite B, Sacramento, CA. 95825. **http://www.bikepolo.com**

Did you know?

That the publisher of the *New York Herald*, James Gordon Bennett, Jr., came back from a European trip in 1876 with a few mallets and balls and an intense interest in the game? He brought some cow ponies up from Texas, gathered some friends, and practiced in Dickel's Riding Academy at 39th and Fifth. In the spring, they moved outdoors to the Jerome Park Race Track in the Bronx. Soon after, the game spread across the United States.

5

SPORTS where you RUN AROUND like a MANIAC

FIELD HOCKEY

HITTING A BALL WITH A STICK IS ABOUT AS BASIC AN INSTINCT AS HITTING A PERSON WITH A STICK. And field hockey (like lacrosse and hurling) provides endless opportunities to do both. The ancient Romans, Arabs, and Persians played a version of field hockey, and you can see a similar game depicted in Egyptian and Greek bas reliefs. There's even evidence that the Aztecs played a game something like it.

Playing

Chelsea Piers (212-336-6500)
West 23rd Street at the West Side Hwy

When there is enough interest, Chelsea sponsors a women's ten-game league open to both individuals and teams.

Greenwich Field Hockey Club
(Call Michael Finnamore at 212-769-9471)

This sports/social club fields two men's teams and one women's, and plays league games in the Northeast Field Hockey Association from October into December. They work out in April, May, and June, then play tournaments around the country, Canada, and the Caribbean in July, August, and September. The men's teams are comprised primarily of ex-pats from some countries where field hockey is most popular (Ireland, England, Germany, Australia). Americans figure more prominently on the women's team. During the winter, the women practice weekdays in Manhattan and play on the weekends in the Bronx. During the summer, they work out during the week on the roof of Trinity School (91st Street and Columbus Avenue). Greenwich organizes a developmental team for those interested in the game who lack experience.

Riverbank State Park (212-694-3600)
On the Hudson River at 145th Street

Offers open field hockey play at various times during the week in-season.

Other Options

There are a number of other field hockey clubs in the area, primarily in Brooklyn and Queens. If you'd like more information about any of them, your best bet is to call the **Northeast Field Hockey Association.** Try Mike Grenhem (home: 973-675-6321, work: 212-297-5390) or Jeff Grosvenor (718-242-5519).

HANDBALL

EW YORK HANDBALL FEATURES LOTS OF ENERGETIC KIDS RUNNING EVERYWHERE AND RETURNING EVERYTHING. But beware of the old men with the big bellies. They don't move, they don't sweat, and they've played this game for 100 years. As a result, they can place shots within three millimeters of anywhere they choose, and that's usually about a quarter-inch past where you can reach.

Outdoors

Almost any schoolyard in the five boroughs.

Carmine Recreation Center (212-242-5228)
Clarkson Street and 7th Avenue South
Some *serious* handball is played here, where you'll find five outdoor courts that are lit for night play.

Central Park Handball Players Association (call Karl Munchow at 749-3710)

North Meadow Recreation Center
West 97th Street about mid-park
Around 120 people who play primarily on weekends from mid-May through mid-October, although some members have been seen shoveling snow off the courts in an attempt to extend the season. No formal teaching is offered, everyone is welcome to play, and informal coaching is easy to come by. The group is comprised of recreational players and a few pros. The oldest active member is 85 years old. The association plays on 12 courts that were constructed in 1938 and are still going strong (just like that 85 year-old.)

Hamilton Fish Recreation Center (212-387-6788)
128 Pitt Street, at Houston Street
Two outdoor courts are available here.

Riverbank State Park (212-694-3600)
On the Hudson River at 145th Street
Four outdoor courts with wooden front walls, available from the beginning of April to the end of November.

Riverside Park (at 72nd and 111th Sts)
Numerous outdoor courts are available.

West 4th Street (and Avenue of the Americas)
Three courts for players here.

Playing Indoors

McBurney YMCA (212-741-9210)
215 West 23rd Street between 7th and 8th Avenues
Three courts for both handball and paddleball.

Vanderbilt YMCA (212-756-9600)
224 East 47th Street between 2nd and 3rd Avenues
No official handball courts, but they play the game against a wall in the gym.

Mayor's Cup Tournament

New York City Sports Commission (212-788-8389). Call for information or an application.

It is estimated that over 700 people in New York regularly compete in handball tournaments, and some 200 of them usually enter this one. The tournament is played at various sites around town over three weekends in June and July. Preliminary matches are held in all five boroughs, and the championship game is usually held on the West 5th Street courts in Coney Island. There are adult male/female and junior male/female categories in both singles and doubles.

Team Handball

This game was invented at the turn of the century by German and Danish soccer players who wanted to stay in shape during the off-season. In Europe, it's second only to soccer in popularity. Even though it has been played in the United States since 1959, many people have never even heard of it. If you're one of those people, team handball combines soccer, basketball, and hockey—and involves running, jumping, catching, and throwing. It's a terrific fast-paced game whose objective is to elude the opposing team by passing a ball quickly from teammate to teammate, then throwing it past a goalie to score.

The New York City Team Handball Club call Ulla Kling Atkinson (212-249-3194, home; or 212-546-2138, work)

The club practices one night a week in Greenpoint, Brooklyn, and is always looking for novice or experienced men and women interested in the game. Men's and women's teams play a September to May schedule, with tournaments starting in January against clubs from Long Island, New Jersey, and Connecticut—continuing once a month until the season is over.

Garden City Handball Club (call Lazlo Yurak at 516-292-8964)

Ideal for experienced players who want to participate at a much higher level, or top-notch athletes interested in taking up the sport. Garden City has won dozens of national championships, and participates in tournaments with other high-level club teams from California, Michigan, Florida, Colorado, Georgia, and elsewhere.

Did you know?

That handball was unknown in this country until around 1882 when Phil Casey, one of Ireland's best players, emigrated to Brooklyn? He soon built a court, opened a school, and, with the help of fellow immigrants from the British Isles, introduced the sport. In 1887 Casey won the first international match ever played, defeating the Irish champion 11 games to six. In fact, he kept his title against all challengers until retiring in 1900.

SOCCER

To say that these men paid their shillings to watch twenty-two hirelings kick a ball is merely to say that a violin is wood and catgut, that Hamlet is so much paper and ink. For a shilling, the Bruddersford United AFC offered you Conflict and Art. —J.B. PRIESTLY, English author and humorist

Playing Outdoors

You can find ferocious weekend pickup games in any of the five boroughs' ethnic communities. You can also try:

East Meadow Central Park, between Fifth Avenue and Park Drive, from 97th Street to 102nd Street

There are pickup games here on in-season weekends, and afternoons after work.

North Meadow Mid-Central Park at about 97th Street

Games on the weekends and some afternoons.

Riverside Park at 103rd Street

There's a new artificial turf, all-weather field here. Looks promising; check it out.

Riverbank State Park (212-694-3600) On the Hudson River at 145th Street

There's a beautiful artificial turf soccer field here. You can get into pickup games on weekday evenings and weekends from the beginning of April through the end of December.

Leagues

Chelsea Piers (212-336-6500) West 23rd Street at the West Side Hwy

Teams play five-on-five on two artificial-turf fields specially built for indoor soccer (and indoor lacrosse). The fields are 110' x 55', surrounded by Plexiglas boards, and equipped with goals, nets, and electronic scoreboards. There are year-round leagues in four divisions: intermediate, competitive, over-30, and women—as well as pickup games. The season runs ten games plus playoffs, and you can join as an individual or with a team.

Cosmopolitan League (Call John Kilby at 201-861-6606)

This league, founded in 1923, is the oldest in North America. It is also the largest by far in the New York area, with some 75 teams throughout all five boroughs (and a few on Long Island as well). Games are played on Sundays throughout the area. The league is divided into three divisions based on ability level, with new teams (only teams can join) usually placed in the third division where they try to work their way up. There is also an over-30 division for all you old wheezers out there.

The New York Metropolitan Women's Soccer League
PO Box 1324, Old Chelsea Station, New York, NY 10113-0925
Contact Diana King at: *NYMWSL@aol.com*
There are usually eight to ten teams in this league which has been promoting and maintaining high-quality women's soccer since its inception in 1978. Their season runs from mid-September through mid-December, then mid-March through the last week of June. The teams play an 18-game schedule, and then participate in State and National Cup tournaments. Comprised primarily of ex-college players, NYMWSL is clearly a playing rather than a teaching league. Home games are played on Sunday afternoons in East River Park.

Reebok (212-362-6800)
160 Columbus Avenue between 67th and 68th Streets
In-season, indoor soccer is played in the gym one weekend afternoon. These games are for members only, and, although informal, the players are quite skilled.

Roosevelt Island Soccer League
(call Ian Walker at 212-274-9740)
This league has two indoor seasons (mid-September through December, and then January through April) and one outdoor (June through August). There are 24 teams competing indoors (five to a side), and all games are played on Roosevelt Island. The outdoor league has 12 teams, 11 to a side, and also plays on the Island. Some Manhattanites seem to think that Roosevelt Island is in another solar system, but it's actually just a subway ride away. Ian will tell you exactly how to get there and reassure you that it's OK to leave your passport at home.

YWCA (212-755-2700)
610 Lexington Avenue at 53rd Street
Runs a coed, indoor soccer league that you can join as an individual or with a team. If you want to join as an individual, you are placed on a team comprised totally of "walk-ons," or on an existing team that needs a player.

A Soccer Club

Barnstonworth Rovers Football Club
(call Paul Grigg at 201-418-9410, or email him at *pgrigg@bellatlantic.net*)
http://home.earthlink.net/~billyw/Rovers/TheClub.html
The Rovers have about 80 members and field one women's team that plays in the Metropolitan League and three men's teams that play in the Cosmopolitan League. One of the men's teams is for those over-30, which plays in a division with other folks from retirement homes. The teams are organized according to ability level—from top competitive to recreational. The season runs from early September through mid-December, then mid-March through the first week of June. They play about 18 games during this time, participate in tournaments, then move indoors in the winter. The men's teams play their home games on Randall's Island and in Central Park; the women's teams in Central and East River Parks. They typically train once a week and play games on Sunday. Two or three new teams are in the planning stages, and they're are always looking for new members. If you're not an absolute beginner, you will be welcome here.

The Urban Street Soccer League

(call Jaime Choy at 212-966-7211)
Never heard of urban street soccer? Well, that's

not surprising because it's a fairly new game that was invented in lower Manhattan. It's played five-on-five plus a goalkeeper, on an asphalt field about one-third regulation size. The games run only 30 minutes, but all the other rules apply. There is a Sunday afternoon league with 12 teams and a Wednesday night league with six teams. The season runs from May to October, and games are played in Sarah D. Roosevelt Park. In the winter, they move the whole shebang indoors to a grade school gym and play four-on-four. Call for more information.

Soccer's Information Central

Soccer Sport Supply (212-427-6050)
1745 First Avenue, between 90th and 91st Streets

This is the place to go for information on the area's leagues, pickup games, and so on. Drop by and talk to Herman. Not only does he sell everything to do with the sport, but he also has an informative bulletin board and can probably hook you up (depending on your skill level) with teams looking for players.

Pro Soccer

MetroStars (888-4-METROTIX)
Giants Stadium, East Rutherford, NJ
http://www.metrostars.com

New Jersey Transit buses (973-762-5100) will get you to the stadium from the Port Authority. The season runs from late-March to late-September.

Minor League Soccer

Long Island Rough Riders (516-756-4625)

Affiliated with the MetroStars, the Rough Riders play a 30 to 35 game schedule against 23 other teams in the A League of the United Systems of Independent Soccer Leagues (the minors of Major League Soccer) from the end of April to the beginning of September.

New York Fever (914-381-5700)

The Fever also play in the USISL, but one rung below the Rough Riders. They also have a summer schedule and typically play their home games at Barrett Stadium (in Westchester Community College, about a 45-minute drive).

New York Magic (914-381-5700)

The Magic play their games during the summer at Barrett Stadium (see above) in the W-League, the first nationwide professional women's soccer league.

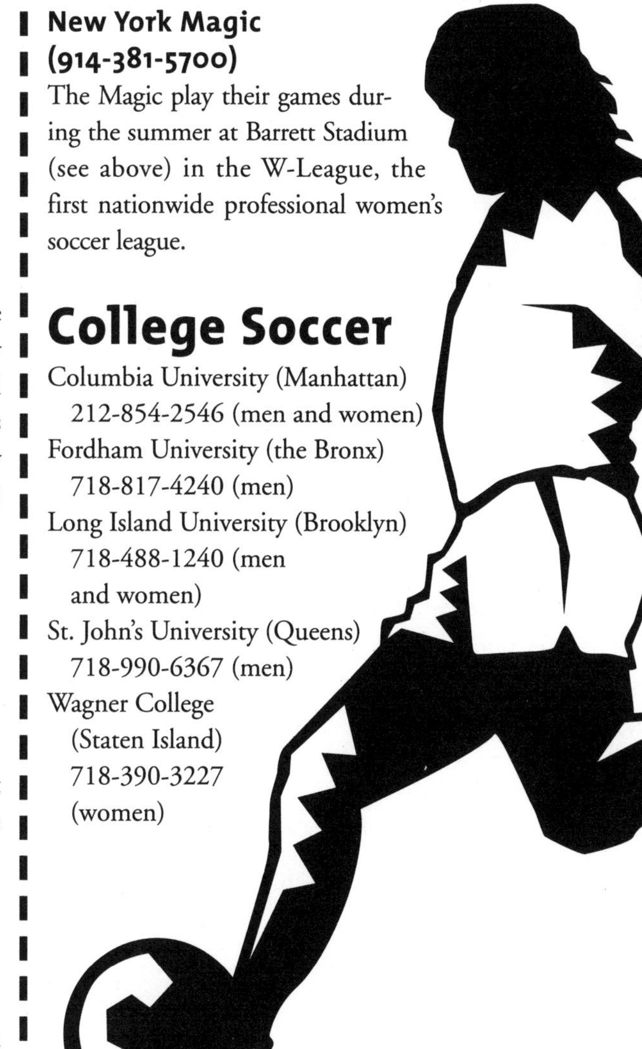

College Soccer

Columbia University (Manhattan)
212-854-2546 (men and women)

Fordham University (the Bronx)
718-817-4240 (men)

Long Island University (Brooklyn)
718-488-1240 (men and women)

St. John's University (Queens)
718-990-6367 (men)

Wagner College (Staten Island)
718-390-3227 (women)

Surfing the Net

The Federation Internationale de Football Association (FIFA) http://wc94.oslonett.no/wc94/fifa.html

Point your browser here for World Cup facts, feature stories, answers to frequently asked questions about soccer, and more.

Did you know?

That, in the fall of 1884, the American Football Association was formed in Newark, New Jersey? Teams were made up mostly of English, Welsh, Scottish, and Irish immigrants, and games were played in vacant lots. Teams prominent at this time were from New York, New Jersey, Philadelphia, and Fall River, Massachusetts.

That the first *recorded* soccer game ever played in this country was in 1886—in Central Park.

ULTIMATE FRISBEE

ONE DAY IN **1957**, the public relations man for the Wham-O Manufacturing Company of San Gabriel, California, saw some Yale students tossing around a metal pie tin. These tins had been produced by Bridgeport, Connecticut's Frisbee Pie Company since 1871. The kids seemed to be having such a good time that Mister P. R. took a tin back with him. From such happy accidents are fortunes made.

Playing and Watching and Learning

Central Park

Weather permitting, pickup games can be found in Central Park's North Meadow (97th Street) on Sunday afternoons from about 2 PM-5 PM, and on Wednesday evenings. Wednesday games start at about 6 PM and end when it's so dark that everyone starts getting plunked in the head. Leagues and teams are always forming or breaking up, so to find out what's doing, go to the park and talk with some of the regulars.

Prospect Park, Brooklyn

There is a mellow game here for beginners and "older folk." Look for it at Long Meadow on Sunday mornings at 10 AM, Tuesday evenings at 6 PM, and on random holiday mornings in the spring and fall. Enter the park at Prospect Park West at 3rd Street and look for the large field in line with 2nd Street.

6
SPORTS
where you gotta be a
TOUGH
GUY

ARM WRESTLING

AYBE YOU'VE ONLY SEEN ARM WRESTLING ON **TV** or in *Over the Top,* that Stallone movie from years ago. But, if you're intrigued, call the **New York Arm Wrestling Association** hotline at 888-544-4592. There's a good chance you'll get Gene (the champ) Camp on the line, whose dedication to the sport has almost single-handedly kept it alive in New York. Gene will put you on his mailing list, and, whether you want to compete or just watch, you'll be notified of all upcoming amateur and professional events.

Every year Gene runs the New York Golden Arms series, which begins with borough-by-borough qualifiers in May and ends in Manhattan in October with the Empire State Tournament of Champions. There are various weight classes for men: 125 lbs. and under, 150 and under, 175 and under, 200 and under, and the super heavyweights at 201 and over; there is also a left-handed super heavyweight class. The two classes for women are 135 lbs. and under, 135 and over. This is a strictly amateur event. No prize money is awarded, but if locker-room bragging rights appeal to you, an arm wrestling title is *very* hard to beat.

BOXING

I want to keep fighting because it's the only thing that keeps me out of the hamburger joints. If I don't fight, I'll eat this planet.

—GEORGE FOREMAN, professional boxer

BOXING IS ONE OF THE OLDEST KNOWN FORMS OF COMPETITION. Although it died out after the fall of Rome, it was revived in England in the early 1700's. Today it occupies first place as the sport that evokes the most powerful cinematic images. You can box within carpeted, air-conditioned splendor, or, if you're a purist, in one of the old-time gyms that smell of sweat, liniment, and dreams.

You should know, however, that just about every sports club in town offers boxing, but usually for its cardiovascular benefits only. This is fine, but if you're interested in contact boxing, call one of the following:

Playing and Watching and Learning

Blue Velvet (822-1960)
23 West 24th Street between 5th and 6th Avenues

This attractive facility (bright and airy, with high ceilings) offers private and semiprivate instruction, with daily, monthly, and yearly memberships. It boasts a top-of-the-line Everlast ring, six heavy bags, three speed, three double-ended, and one upper-cut bag. About 20% of the members are professional fighters (and celebrities), and the rest are recreational boxers and amateurs. Many Blue Velvet instructors have world-class credentials, including Victor Machado, who trained 12 world champions; Vito Antuofermo, former middleweight champion of the world; Iran Barkley, three-time world champion, and Jimmy Glenn, who founded the fabled Times Square Gym and ran it for over 18 years. There are locker rooms and showers for men and women, plus free weights and exercise gear downstairs.

Chelsea Piers (212-336-6000)
West 23rd Street at the West Side Highway

Chelsea has a full-size ring plus heavy and speed bags. They offer private and semiprivate lessons, plus a boxing school that will move you through three levels of proficiency. Carlos Ortiz is advertised as an instructor, so if you want to get your nose bloodied by a former, world junior welterweight champion, drop by. They also offer kick-boxing.

Church Street Boxing Gym
(212-571-1333 and 212-962-5046)
25 Park Place, between Church Street and Broadway

"This Isn't Pretty" is the gym motto, but pretty or not, it's the largest boxing-only facility in town. This gym provides two rings, 25 heavy, eight speed, and four double-ended bags. The trainers here are first-rate. They're all licensed by the New York State Athletic Commission and all have extensive experience with professional fighters. But don't be put off by that because they'll work with you at whatever level or pace you want. The crowd here is very mixed: men and women (with locker rooms for each—plus a sauna), white collar types, serious amateurs, and pros. You can pay daily, monthly, or yearly,

and if you're thinking about making a career change, the fee for competitive boxers is $10 less a month than for you and me. Church Street also puts on the Friday Night Fights, which feature some of the best amateur boxers from NYC and the surrounding areas.

Crunch (212-614-0120)
404 Lafayette Street, between Astor Place and East 4th Street

Facilities include a boxing studio with a ring, six heavy, two double-ended, and four speed bags. Instruction is available in all the basics. You can either join the club, or buy a day pass if you just want to try it out. This Crunch facility (and a few other Crunches) also offers kickboxing.

Gleason's (718-797-2872)
75 Front Street, Brooklyn Heights (right under the Brooklyn Bridge)

A little while ago we had two originals in town: Julian's pool hall and Gleason's Gym. Julian's is gone but Gleason's remains—maybe the most famous gym in the country. It has over 60 trainers and about 650 members, seven of whom are world champions. Once a month there's a White Collar Sparring contest open to the 400 or so men and women members who do something other than box for a living. You can pay yearly, monthly, or daily here—and they don't charge a penny extra for the authentic atmosphere.

Kingsway Boxing Center (212-679-3427)
1 West 28th Street between 5th Avenue and Broadway

Offers two rings, six heavy, four speed, and two double-ended bags, plus two "No Spitting in the Gym" signs. Also available are exercise equipment and weights, and private and group instruction. The gym draws a very mixed coed crowd of pros, amateurs, and recreational fighters, and is certainly on the authentic rather than yuppie side of the dividing line.

Printing House Fitness and Racquet Club (212-243-7600)
421 Hudson Street at Leroy Street

This is a members-only club with a boxing ring, six heavy bags, four speed, three uppercut, and one double-ended bag. They offer private and semiprivate instruction at all levels.

World Gym (212-780-7407)
232 Mercer Street between Bleecker and West 3rd Streets

World Gym has a ring and various speed and heavy bags, and offers boxing instruction for members at various levels, as well as in group, semiprivate, and private settings.

Did you know?

That the longest boxing match on record was seven hours and 19 minutes? It went 110 rounds and was fought in New Orleans in April of 1893, and after all that, Andy Bowen and Jack Burke fought to a draw.

That the shortest match was a November, 1947 Golden Glove bout fought in Minneapolis? Mike Collins floored Pat Brownson with the very first punch he threw. The fight was stopped after four seconds.

FOOTBALL

When I played pro football, I never set out to hurt anybody deliberately unless it was, you know, important, like a league game or something.

—DICK BUTKUS, former professional football player

Playing and Watching

East Meadow
Central Park, between Fifth Avenue and Park Drive, from 97th to 102nd Streets

Pickup games take place in-season on the weekends and some afternoons after work.

North Meadow
Mid-Central Park, at about 97th Street

You can usually find pickup games on in-season weekends and afternoons.

Riverbank State Park (212-694-3600)
Hudson River at 145th Street

The park has a beautiful, artificial turf football field with lights. You can participate in touch and flag pickup games on weekday evenings and on weekends, from the end of August through the end of December.

Leagues

Big Apple Flag Football League
(Call Rich DeCicco or Jack Morris at 718-268-1208)

Active in Manhattan and Queens, the league has 40 teams in two divisions. The A League is a bit more competitive than the B League: you can rush the passer as soon as the ball is snapped, but in the B League, pass rushers have to count "one Mississippi, two Mississippi" before they can go after the quarterback. There are nine games plus playoffs and a championship game in each of three seasons: fall (September through December), winter (January through March), and spring (March through June.) What's most fun about Big Apple is its championship game, which is usually held in a major stadium (the last few at Giants Stadium). The league welcomes both individuals and teams.

Yorkville Sports Association
(212-645-6488)
http://home.earthlink.net/~ysa/

Runs men's, women's and coed touch-football leagues starting in early September. You must be 21 or older, and you must enter with a team. It's a ten-game season plus playoffs, and games are played on weekends in Central Park, Randall's Island, and other Manhattan locations.

United Football League (212-252-3555)

This is a semipro league that operates in the tristate area. There are four divisions with 24 teams, and the Bronx, Queens, Brooklyn, and Manhattan are represented. The league plays a ten-game schedule. Although the games are funded by the players themselves, sponsors are always sought. United also has playoffs, a championship game, and an All-Star game.

YWCA (212-755-2700)
610 Lexington Avenue at 53rd Street
Sponsors a flag football league, which begins in the fall with games on weekday evenings.

Pro Football

Giants (201-935-8111)
Giants Stadium, East Rutherford, NJ
http://www.nfl.com/giants/
Season tickets are almost impossible to obtain: They are left to children in wills, are hotly contested over in divorces. Over 25,000 names appear on the waiting list. So, snuggle up in front of your TV, get invited by someone luckier than you, or take your chances with a scalper. New Jersey Transit buses (973-762-5100) from the Port Authority will get you there.

Jets (516-560-8100)
Meadowlands, East Rutherford, New Jersey
http://www.nfl.com/jets/
Yes, when the Giants play it's called Giants Stadium, but until the Jets build a field of their own, they just change the name of the field to the Meadowlands. Jets games, too, have been sold out for years, and there are 10,000 names on their season's ticket waiting list. Although it's rare, if you wait until after the kickoff, you may find a scalper who's willing to take *something* for a ticket instead of getting completely burned.

Arena Football

The Cityhawks (212-465-2489)
Madison Square Garden, 7th Avenue between 31st and 33rd Streets
http://www.ipsnews.com/cityhawks
Arena football was invented around 12 years ago during a soccer match at Madison Square Garden. If you've never seen a game, it's a real experience. The field is small, and the action is aggressive and nonstop. Eight players on each side busily knock into each other and into the padded walls surrounding the field: Any ball that caroms off the taut nets stretched behind each goal post is in play. The Cityhawks play from the end of April to the end of July, with playoffs in August. There are usually tickets available for all home games.

The Red Dogs (201-507-1303)
Continental Arena, East Rutherford, NJ
The Red Dogs is the Jersey entrant in the Arena Football League.

College Football:

Columbia University (Manhattan) 212-854-2546
Fordham University (the Bronx) 718-817-4240
St. John's University (Queens) 718-990-6367
Wagner College (Staten Island) 718-390-3227

Australian Rules Football

This game was started by Australian gold miners who worked 12-hour shifts and still had enough energy left over to run around knocking the bejesus out of each other. It's a cross between rugby and Gaelic football, and is a must for those of you who think those two games are for wimps. Besides, how could you not love a game that's called *footy* by its fans? No Australian Rules Football club exists in the New York area at the moment, but if Erik Kallhovd has his way this will all change (home: 914-289-0145, work: 914-694-9300). Erik is trying to stir up enough interest to form a club to compete with those in Kansas City, St. Louis, Washington D.C., and California. And you have to love Erik. He said to me, "If *those* places can have a team, then we can certainly have one."

Did you know?

That the first college football game was played in New Brunswick, New Jersey in 1869 between Princeton and Rutgers? There were 25 men on each side, and running with the ball was forbidden.

That a sort of football world series was played in 1902 and 1903 inside Madison Square Garden?

That Tim Mara bought the New York Giants franchise for $500? He said: "*Any* New York franchise is worth $500."

HURLING AND GAELIC FOOTBALL

IN HURLING, WHICH IS THE IRISH NATIONAL GAME, fifteen players a side use wooden sticks to smack a ball and each other up and down a field (two parts lacrosse, three parts field hockey, and five parts aggression). The action is nonstop, and to say that tempers flare demeans the concept of being angry.

Gaelic football is a rugby-like affair with running, kicking, and jumping. Helmets and pads do little to stop the bone-jarring tackles and full-speed collisions. The game began in the 1500's with 25 to 100 men lined up at the midway point between two different towns. The winning team had to drive the ball across the other town's boundary. Needless to say, neither of these games is for the faint of heart. (And neither is the woman's version of hurling, called *camogie.*)

If you'd like to check them out, both seasons run from the first Sunday in April through the end of October. The games are played (and have been since the 1920's) in **Gaelic Park,** at Broadway and 240th Street in the Bronx. There are four games every Sunday starting at 1 PM, and you can spend the entire day watching men's, women's, junior's, and senior's hurling and football games.

And if you get hooked enough to have a favorite team, you can follow their exploits in either of our two main Irish weeklies: the *Irish Echo* or the *Irish Voice.*

LACROSSE

They thought lacrosse was what you find in la church.

—ROBIN WILLIAMS, comedian and actor

ORIGINALLY A NATIVE AMERICAN GAME IN WHICH UPWARDS OF 2000 PLAYERS TOOK PART, lacrosse was considered great training for war because each player tried to disable as many opponents as possible. The goals were set miles apart and a game could last three days or more. (Am I crazy, or does this sound exactly like trying to get out of town for the 4th of July weekend?)

Playing Indoors

Chelsea Piers (212-336-6500) West 23rd Street at the West Side Highway

Sponsors year-round leagues for both men and women. There's no checking allowed in the indoor game, and the women (who play without gloves, pads, and helmets) use a physical barrier instead of a person to protect the goal. The two artificial-turf fields at Chelsea were specially built for indoor lacrosse (and indoor soccer). They are 110' x 55,' surrounded by Plexiglas boards, and equipped with goals, nets, and electronic scoreboards. Chelsea provides referees, game balls, and league jerseys, and you can join as an individual or with a team. The season lasts ten games plus playoffs, and matches are typically played on Sundays (women from 4 PM to 6 PM, and men from 6 PM to 9 PM).

Pro Lacrosse

The New York Saints (516-794-9303) Nassau Veterans Memorial Coliseum in Uniondale, Long Island

The Saints play in the National Lacrosse League, and have a 14-game schedule that runs from the beginning of January through mid-April (with playoffs extending into May). The league currently has eight teams (New York, Boston, Philadelphia, Baltimore, Syracuse, Rochester, Hamilton, and Buffalo).

College Lacrosse

Columbia University (Manhattan) 212-854-2546

Wagner College (Staten Island) 718-390-3227

RUGBY

I prefer rugby to soccer. When soccer players start biting each other's ears off, maybe I'll like it better. —ELIZABETH TAYLOR, actress

IF YOU'RE INTERESTED IN A SPORT THAT BOASTS BUMPER STICKERS SAYING "Give Blood, Play Rugby," which is played in over 100 countries and ranks fourth worldwide in numbers of participants, and which allows players to cheerfully smash into each other without the protection of helmets or pads (as in Gaelic and Australian Rules Football), then knock yourself out (literally) and call one of these clubs:

Playing and Watching

Manhattan Rugby Club (212-802-4754)

Founded in 1960, this is one of the top clubs in the Northeast. Their home field is on Randall's Island, and they play in the Premier League, traveling from Boston to Washington D.C. (and beyond) for games. The club fields two competitive sides plus an "old boys" team. They practice twice weekly and play games every weekend March through May, then September through November. In the summer, they play sevens (seven players to a side). Both a social and a playing club, it always welcomes new members.

New York Rugby Football Club (212-988-9201)

This is the oldest rugby club in the country and the only one in the metropolitan area that fields both a men's and women's side. NYRFC was founded in 1929 as the New York Nomads and played its first match in the spring of 1930. The club plays very competitive rugby and welcomes anyone interested in joining as a playing or social member. The club plays its home games on various fields on Randall's Island and usually engages in a fitness session during the week. The club hosts a one-day sevens tournament each November, with games on Randall's and Ward's Island. The tournament has five divisions: premier, club, collegiate, social, and women's. Some 100 teams usually participate, coming from as far away as Lithuania, Holland, Venezuela, and Hong Kong.

Old Blue (212-477-6171)

Founded about 30 years ago on the campus of Columbia University, this club has become one of the tops in the country. You should know before you call that Old Blue plays *very* competitive rugby. Although beginners are welcome and informal coaching is available, this is much more of a playing than a social club. The season begins in early September and runs through the end of October, then starts again at the end of March and runs through the end of May. There are about 50 active members. This all adds up to about a 20-game schedule, but the club also participates in tournaments on the East coast and further afield. During the off-season, Old Blue plays sevens, and trains twice weekly at Baker's Field (218th Street and Broadway). Home matches are played in Van Cortlandt Park (252nd Street and Broadway).

The Village Lions (212-631-3533)
In existence since 1989, and sanctioned by both USA Rugby and the Metropolitan New York Rugby Union, this club plays pretty serious rugby. The club roster includes players from eight different countries. On average, all players have over five years of experience with the sport. The club currently has about 50 members, and new ones are always welcome. The Lions practice in East River Park (off Houston) and play a 12-game schedule on Randall's Island. Their season runs from late March to mid-June, and includes various tournaments throughout the East Coast.

WRESTLING

I believe professional wrestling is clean and everything else in the world is fixed.

—FRANK DEFORD, sportswriter and novelist

THERE IS NO SPORT OLDER NOR MORE UNIVERSAL THAN WRESTLING. With roots in hand-to-hand combat, the sport evolved to the point where "I give" was substituted for getting killed. There are wrestling scenes in 3,000-year-old Babylonian and Egyptian works of art. Hulk Hogan and Macho Man Randy Savage aside, this is one of the original *unmovable object vs. irresistible force* sports. If you remember wrestling from high school gym class, you probably also remember that it made you more tired than you ever thought possible. You had to go all out every second, and push/pull someone who was pushing/pulling you. If this memory is from the "don't ever mention the word wrestling again" file, read no further. But if "that was a pretty good workout" comes to mind, you have some options.

Learning

Crunch (212-614-0120)
404 Lafayette Street, between Astor Place and East 4th Street
Offers a wrestling class designed for beginners. There are drills to acquire strength and mobility (sort of a cardiovascular tune-up), plus all the traditional takedown and pinning moves.

Knights Wrestling Club
(Contact Ed Unger, 212-627-1921)
The club has been offering instruction and competition in the gay and lesbian communities since 1981. Members workout Saturday afternoons at the Lesbian and Gay Community Center (212-620-7310, 208 West 13th Street between 7th and 8th Avenues) and welcome anyone who'd like to learn the sport or already has

some experience and is interested in advancing to the next level. The Knights team participates in various tournaments, competes with clubs from Philadelphia, Washington D.C., and Boston, and has won championships at the Gay Games.

West Side YMCA (212-749-3404) 5 West 63rd, between Central Park West and Broadway

A great place for organized workouts and informal instruction, this Y is home to one of the oldest adult wrestling programs in New York, and regulars sometimes compete in tournaments and against local colleges.

College Wrestling

Columbia University (Manhattan) 212-854-2546
Wagner College (Staten Island) 718-390-3227

> **Did you know?**
> **That on April 30, 1898, Ernest Roeber and Ismael Yousoff (the Terrible Turk) squared off in a championship wrestling match on the stage of the Metropolitan Opera House? After 20 minutes or so, the two began to slug it out—and the fans soon joined the fun.**

SPORTS where you HAVE TO be CRAZY (A LITTLE)

7

HANG GLIDING AND PARAGLIDING

HANG GLIDING CAME ON THE SCENE IN THE 1960'S. The glider itself was adapted from the design of a NASA engineer named Francis Rogallo, who developed a fixed-wing parachute to help steer space vehicles upon reentry into the atmosphere.

Paragliding began in 1978 with skydivers in the French Alps who were tired of waiting for the next airplane, the right weather conditions, and the constant repacking of their parachutes. One day they opened their chutes, ran down a mountainside, got airborne, and started a new sport.

Since these two sports can be very dangerous, be sure to ask about the qualifications of the instructors, and then follow your instincts about where you think you'll be most comfortable and safest.

Learning and Gliding

Fly High Hang Gliding (914-744-3317)
5163 Searsville Road, Pine Bush, NY

(about a two-hour drive from town)

These folks make the point that skydiving is as safe as downhill skiing and scuba diving. If you don't view this as safe enough, perhaps you should find something a bit less adventurous. But if you're undeterred, Fly High gets you started in a two-person tandem glider with an instructor. You can graduate to a three tandem-flight package or a package of training hill lessons (two hours of field instruction and four hours of solo.) After that, you can arrange for advanced lessons, and buy and store a glider. To arrange for a lesson, call a week in advance.

You can also paraglide at Fly High, and ride the same air currents as the hang gliders. Paragliders weigh 25 pounds and fold into a backpack. Instruction and storage are available, and you can also purchase equipment.

Mountain Wings Hang Gliding Center (914-647-3377)
150 Canal Street, Ellenville, NY

(just under two hours away)

In business since 1981, Mountain Wings operates at the foot of Ellenville Mountain, where the hang-gliding distance record is 98 miles, and the duration record is 11-1/2 hours. The facility is open year-round and is certified by the United States Hang Gliding Association. Choose from among a one-day introductory program (a morning ground school and an afternoon of gliding), a six-day novice program, and an eagle program (up to ten days of preparation for two high-altitude flights). Private, semiprivate, and group lessons are available. If you just want to give hang gliding a try without really working at it, you can sign up for a tandem flight with an experienced instructor. No experience is necessary, and there are no age restrictions. However, there's a 210-pound limit. So if you weigh more, you'll have to drop some weight or find another way to scare the bejesus out of yourself.

You can also paraglide here and sign up for a one-day introduction, or a take-off program that gives you as many lessons as you need to reach USHGA Class 1 status. There's also a Class 2 program (one day of theory, one day of flying, a written exam); a Class 3 program (advanced aerodynamics, advanced meteorology, a written exam), and additional offerings leading to Class 4 and 5 status.

PARASAILING

SO IT'S LIKE THIS: YOU GET ON A BOAT AND STRAP INTO A PARACHUTE-HARNESS-AND-SEAT-TYPE-THING. The parachute is attached to a cable, and, as the boat accelerates, the staff slowly unwind it until you're up around 300 feet. And there you drift, accompanied by the sound of the wind, and a spectacular view of the city, Staten Island, and even the Jersey shore. If you think this sounds like a terrifying ten minutes, I don't blame you; but if it sounds like a kick, you can mosey over to **ParaSail New York** at the North Cove Yacht Center (212-691-0055, on the river at the World Financial Center, Liberty Street and South End Avenue). You can parasail by yourself or with a friend, and you won't even get wet because they slowly crank you down to the same deck.

No special skill (except nerve) is required. The season runs from May through October, and, as their brochure points out, you can even wear a suit: business, bathing, or birthday.

ROCK CLIMBING

Sooner or later you're going to be looking at God saying, "We're going to be lucky if we get out of here." Your life is going to be in front of you and then you are going to realize that you'd rather be grocery shopping. —ED BARRY, climber

THE GUNKS, IN THE SHAWANGUNK MOUNTAINS OF NEW PALTZ, NEW YORK, is the premier rock-climbing site in the Northeast. And since it's only a few hours away, New York City has a small but growing group of climbers who can do their thing indoors as well as out.

Indoors

Chelsea Piers

West 23rd Street at the West Side Hwy

You have two choices here. If you're a beginner and just want to give the sport a try, go to the climbing wall in the Field House (212-336-6500). This wall is 26' x 55' and is a good place for an introduction. Start off with a few classes to see if climbing's for you. The other option is the wall at the Sports Center (212-366-6000, memberships and day passes). This is an awesome sight. The wall is 46' x 180' and has over 10,000 square feet of climbing surface. The surface itself is made of polymer with granite inlay (so it really feels like rock). In addition, there is a specially designed 25' overhang, which is amazing to watch people climb. The routes here are changed all the time, and if you're not already experienced, the entire affair looks diabolical. There is also an adjacent 10' x 73' bouldering wall (which you climb across rather than scale up). Chelsea offers rental equipment and private and semiprivate instruction at various levels, plus top roping and belayer certification classes.

ExtraVertical Climbing Center
(212-586-5382)
Harmony Atrium, Broadway, between 62nd and 63rd Street

This is a great spot for climbing enthusiasts who also love an audience. The facility is located right off the sidewalk in a large, open space, and there's almost always a crowd gathered to watch the action. Some 2200 square feet of climbing surface is spread over 30' and 50' walls. Lessons are available for every skill level, and equipment can be rented or purchased.

Manhattan Plaza Health Club
(212-563-7001)
482 West 43rd Street at 10th Avenue

The club has a 20' wall with over 2,000 square feet of climbing surface and 35 routes to the top. The staff redesigns the wall every month to keep the challenges interesting. Annual fee and drop-in arrangements can be made, and clinics, workshops, and seminars for beginners and intermediates are available. You can also rent gear.

Reebok
(212-758-6800)
160 Columbus Avenue, between 67th and 68th Streets

Club members have use of a 40' wall. Instruction (private and semiprivate) is available at various skill levels, and the club also offers a ropes course. As an added bonus, this wall is probably a good place to get discovered. It seems like every time I'm there, a video crew is shooting a commercial, or a still photographer is shooting an ad.

Indoors/ Outdoors

North Meadow Recreation Center
(212-348-4867)
Mid-Central Park on the north side of 97th Street

Offers a 12-hour program designed for beginners or for climbers who want to refresh their skills. It covers balance, weight shifting, traversing, knot tying, rope handling, and belaying. Classes are held on both indoor and outdoor climbing walls. The indoor wall is very small and suited for basic instruction in grips and techniques, and the outdoor is 25' with grips attached to a vertical concrete slab. There is also an intermediate program, with sessions in Fort Tryon Park. Here, climbers tackle a 50' wall of the Cloisters: a granite rock face with natural cracks and overhangs.

Outdoors

Rat Rock
Mid-Central Park at 63rd Street, just south of the softball fields

Chess Rock
Central Park, just north of the Wollman Rink

Clubs

City Climbers Club (212-974-2250)
533 West 59th Street, between 10th and 11th Avenues

The city's only rock-climbing club has an indoor climbing wall that, although not large, offers challenging and imaginative routes to the top. And since the club is run by and for climbers, they also have maps of the best climbing spots, including Rat and Chess Rocks.

SKYDIVING

IT ONLY *SEEMS* THAT LEONARDO DA VINCI INVENTED EVERYTHING IN THE WORLD, but he did actually invent the parachute. And although he made the original design sketches, it was a certain Louis-Sebastien Lenormand who put the principle into practice: In 1783 he jumped out of a tree holding two very large parasols.

You obviously can't skydive right here in town, but you can choose from among a number of jump schools in the area. And although many use different lingo, they all teach essentially the same thing. You usually start off with a tandem jump (following a preliminary training session), during which you're be attached to an instructor in a parachute-built-for-two. After a short freefall, you pull the ripcord and float down, secure in the knowledge that if you freak out completely, you're not alone. These tandem jumps familiarize you with the basics. A certain number of them are usually required before you're allowed to advance.

After ground training on flying and landing a parachute, certain schools then move you to static line jumps: A line attached to the plane opens your chute, and a ground radio guides you down.

Other schools move from tandem to advanced freefall. This includes a jump in the company of instructors, during which you get a real taste of hurtling through the air. After a certain number of freefalls, you're ready to move on.

Accelerated freefall is the most advanced training. You progress to higher and higher altitudes, with longer and longer freefalls.

Since skydiving is always dependent on the weather, you can't be assured that you'll jump the same day you train. Always ask about the instructor's qualifications, and go where you're most comfortable—even if it means driving a few more miles.

Learning and Jumping

Duanesburg Skydiving School (518-895-8140) Duanesburg, NY

(about 2-1/2 hours away)

These folks have been in business for nearly 25 years. They do tandem jumps, followed by four hours of training, and then static line jumps from 4,000'. Then it's another four hours of training until you can try an accelerated freefall from 11,000' (with two instructors, and 45 seconds of freefall).

Sky's the Limit (800-335-JUMP) Orange County Airport, Montgomery, NY

(just under fifty miles away)

Sky's the Limit operates six days a week in April, and daily May through mid-November. There is ground instruction and then three tandem jumps from 10,000' to 14,000'. To advance, it's ten jumps of advanced freefall, and then eight levels of accelerated freefall.

Sky Dive Long Island (516-878-5867) Montauk Highway, East Moriches, NY

(near the Hamptons, about 2-1/2 hours away)

Classroom instruction is offered concerning how to exit, how to maneuver, how to land, and what to do in case of an emergency. Then there's practical ground training. You're allowed to go up only when your instructor thinks you're ready, and then it's static line jumps as you progress. You can also choose to start with a tandem jump from about a mile up.

Sky Dive the Ranch (914-255-4033) Gardiner, NY (about 1-1/2 hours away)

Instruction is offered every day of the week. This is a skydiving club as well as school, so if you get hooked, you can stay hooked. If you're already an experienced jumper and want more information about the club only, call 914-255-9538. For beginners, it's ground instruction and then tandem jumps, with about a minute of freefall followed by seven levels of accelerated freefall. Levels 1 through 3 are taught by two instructors, and Levels 4 through 7 by one instructor.

Skydive Sussex (973-702-7000) Route 639, Sussex, NJ (48 miles from town)

Offers a two-hour canopy control class: two tandem jumps from two-miles up. Next, it's four hours of class and then seven levels of accelerated freefall. Two instructors accompany you during the first two levels and one instructor accompanies you for the rest.

Note: If you're getting the impression that I think anyone who hang glides, paraglides, parasails, rock climbs, or skydives is nuts, please understand that I can't even step on the first rung of a very short ladder without my heart pounding like the drum section of Grambling's marching band. One day I'll tell you the story about my being frozen on a ledge at some Anasazi ruins in New Mexico. So what this is *really* all about is that I'm envious and very respectful of all you "up in the air" types.

8

SPORTS where you have to be LAZY (A LOT)

FANTASY & VIRTUAL REALITY SPORTS

THERE ARE FANTASY LEAGUES FOR JUST ABOUT EVERY SPORT YOU CAN THINK OF. You can even play e-mail cricket. They're not included in this book because I believe you have to move at least one set of muscles to play a sport, and moving a pen across paper or fingers across a keyboard just doesn't qualify for me. Therefore, it might seem like a contradiction that I've included **XS New York.** But I don't see it that way. After all, you have to get up, get out, and get there.

XS New York

(212-398-5467)
Broadway at 42nd Street

"Too Much Is Not Enough" is the motto at New York's premier high-tech, multilevel, interactive, virtual game arena. With rock music blaring in the background here are your options: You can pretend you're snowboarding or snow skiing, make believe you're hang gliding or playing golf, dream you're skateboarding or kicking soccer balls, imagine you're jet skiing or shooting hoops, or fantasize that you're pitching a baseball game. All this is in addition to the usual arcade games where you're invited to kill aliens, crash cars, race motorcycles, drive tanks, and kick the asses of various Kung Fu fighters.

And that's not all. Downstairs, you can put on a special vest, pick up a "lazer" gun, and play an eight-minute game of tag in a darkened maze. You get hit, your vest buzzes, and you're dead.

Net-net, I prefer not to think of XS as a wave of the future, but rather, as an interesting exercise in technology and computer graphics, and as a gift from the gods should you ever be faced with 12 little kids, a birthday party, and a rainy day.

9
SPORTS
with
RACQUETS
and
PADDLES

BADMINTON

TWO NEW YORKERS INTRODUCED BADMINTON TO THIS COUNTRY, and even though they first saw the game in two different places (Bayard Clark in England and E. Langdon Wilkes in India) they hooked up here in the winter of 1878 and formed the Badminton Club of New York, the *first* badminton club in the United States.

Playing and Watching and Learning

Badminton Club of the City of New York
plays on Saturdays from 11 AM to 2 PM, October through March, on five courts at Julia Richman High School (68th Street and 2nd Avenue). They welcome new members, but you must be sponsored by a current member to join. So go over there one Saturday morning in whites and court shoes, play as their guest, and get acquainted.

Brooklyn Badminton Club
(Norris Johnson at 718-332-9032)
This club plays one to two days a week in the Roosevelt Hall Extension Gym at Brooklyn College (2900 Bedford Street, between Avenue I and Campus Road). The club welcomes players at all levels, and instruction is available. They will loan you a racquet if you're just starting out, but these racquets have seen better days, and you'll want to buy your own very quickly. Their season runs from the end of September to the end of May, and you can either pay yearly dues or drop-in fees.

Central Manhattan Badminton Club
(Abby Colotelo at 212-831-0302,
or David Folds at 212-274-3023)
Central Manhattan plays one evening a week from September to the end of May at Robert Wagner Junior High (76th Street between 2nd and 3rd Avenues). This is a club for folks who already know how to play the game. There are four courts at the school, drop-ins are welcome, and there are annual dues plus a nightly fee.

Humanities High School
351 West 18th Street between 8th
and 9th Avenues
This isn't a formal club, team, or league, but simply a gathering of people who enjoy badminton. The schedule can vary depending on the number of people playing and the needs of the school, so call Chibing Woo at 718-205-0987 for the latest. Instruction is available.

Surfing the Net

The United States
Badminton Association
http://mid1.external.hp.
com/stanb/badminton.html
Loaded with facts, figures, training tips, listings of worldwide organizations, current events, tournaments, and links to other badminton sites.

PADDLEBALL

PADDLEBALL BECAME POPULAR HERE IN THE 1850'S, and as New Yorkers moved elsewhere, they took the game with them. It's now played throughout the country and as far away as Israel and Japan. Paddleball is a real city game because you don't need a lot of space or a lot of stuff. If you have a wall, a ball, and a paddle, then you can have a game. There are about 10,000 courts in the city (in nearly every park and playground), and an estimated 100,000 players. The sport has recently enjoyed a large surge in popularity, due to strong interest in the Latino and African-American communities.

Playing and Watching

Carmine Recreation Center
(212-242-5228)
Clarkson Street and 7th Avenue South
The five outdoor courts are lit for night play. And the times I've stopped by, there was *serious* paddleball being played here.

North Meadow Recreation Center
Mid-Central Park at West 97th Street
Twelve outdoor courts can be found here.

Riverbank State Park (212-694-3600)
Hudson River at 145th Street
Four outdoor courts with *wooden* front walls. Open from the beginning of April to the end of November.

Riverside Park (at 111th Street)
Has 12 outdoor courts.

West 4th Street (and Avenue of the Americas)
Has three courts.

Associations

The National Paddleball Association
373 Park Avenue South, 10th Floor,
New York, NY 10016
http://www.paddleball.com/NPA/MEMBERSH.html
Runs singles and doubles tournaments in the city during May, June, and July. One of the tournaments is the New York City Open, which progresses from Coney Island, to Queens, to the Bronx, and winds up in Central Park. A second is the Pro-Am Men's Doubles, which is played at Coney Island and Orchard Beach. Both tourneys have drawn players from Connecticut, New Jersey, Florida, and the U.S. Virgin Islands. Members pay annual dues and receive schedules and announcements, a T-shirt, discounts on tickets, fees, gear, and more.

PADDLE TENNIS

ADDLE TENNIS SHOULDN'T BE CONFUSED WITH PLATFORM TENNIS (the one you play on an elevated platform encased in chicken wire). This game is played on a court about half-regulation size, using a solid or perforated paddle (that is, no strings), and a deadened tennis ball (just think of a standard ball punctured by a needle). You are allowed only one underhand serve, but the rest is like regular tennis, from the grips and strokes, to the strategies and scoring. Paddle tennis emphasizes net play and is a game of fast returns and long rallies.

The place to go for info about this sport is the United States Paddle Tennis Association, and the man to speak with is Jack Heller (718-894-7728). The USPTA is a nonprofit organization established in 1923, and it's also the governing body of the sport. The organization runs free clinics and sponsors tournaments, typically in May, June, July, and September.

Playing and Watching

MANHATTAN

East River Park
FDR Drive, just south of the Williamsburg Bridge
There are multiple courts, but only two are really usable.

Peter Cooper Village
North side of 20th Street, one block from the East River
There are three courts.

Stuyvesant Town
14th Street and Avenue B
South side of 20th, one block from the East River
There are three courts at each location.

BROOKLYN

Commodore Barry Park
Near the Navy Yard, between Park Avenue, Navy Street, Flushing Avenue, and North Eliot Place
One court is available here.

Neptune Playground
Neptune Avenue and West 12th Street
Three courts.

QUEENS

Jacob Riis Park
About Beach 160th in the Rockaways
There are four courts.

LONG ISLAND

Jones Beach
Fifteen courts in the Center Mall, at Parking Field Four. And while you're there, you can eat at the Boardwalk Restaurant and play either miniature golf or Pitch and Putt. (For Jones Beach information, call 516-785-1600).

SQUASH AND RACQUETBALL

Squash is boxing with racquets.

—JONAH BARRINGTON, English squash champion

Squash probably originated at Harrow, England, sometime before 1850 with students who had taken to hitting a soft India-rubber ball against a wall. The ball looked as if it squashed when it hit the wall, hence the name of the sport.

Racquet ball was invented in 1950 by a man named Joe Sobek from the Greenwich, Connecticut YMCA. He combined squash and handball to form "paddle racquets," and the game took off from there.

Playing

Club La Raquette (212-245-1144)
Parker Meridien Hotel, 119 West 56th Street between 6th and 7th Avenues
This is a 15,000 square-foot, full-service health club that was completely renovated in 1996 and has twice made *Fitness* magazine's "top ten health clubs in New York" list. The club has one squash and two racquetball courts for club members, their guests, and hotel guests. Although day passes are available, this gets expensive fast, so a membership probably makes sense if you fall in love with the place. Private lessons are available, and there are challenge courts, ladders, and spring and fall tournaments.

New York Health & Racquet Club
110 West 56th Street at 6th Avenue
(212-541-7200)
Two racquetball courts.

20 East 50th Street between 5th and Madison Avenues (212-593-1500)
Two squash courts.

39 Whitehall Street between Pearl and Water Streets (212-422-4653)
Two racquetball and three squash courts.
NYHRC courts are for the use of members and their guests, and additional fees are charged for court time and lessons (private, semiprivate, and group). There are, however, free clinics plus leagues and tournaments.

New York Sports Clubs
151 East 86th Street at Lexington Avenue
(212-860-8630)
Four squash courts.

61 West 62nd Street at Broadway
(212-265-0995)
Three squash courts.

404 5th Avenue at 37th Street
(212-594-3120)
Two squash courts.
New York Sports Club allows the public to pay a daily fee to use their squash courts, but they're primarily intended for club members. Instruction is available at all levels.

Printing House Fitness and Racquet Club (212-243-7600)

421 Hudson Street at Leroy Street
A members-only club, this is one of the best squash facilities in town with six squash courts, round robin tournaments, clinics on strokes and strategy, and individual instruction at all levels. They also have a player matching service.

Vertical Club (212-255-5100)
330 East 61st Street between 1st and 2nd Avenues

The club has two squash and four racquetball courts for members and their guests. The club offers clinics and tournaments, and private and group lessons can be arranged.

West Side Y
(212-787-4400)
5 West 63rd Street between Central Park West and Broadway

The Y has two squash courts that members can reserve up to three days in advance for singles and doubles. There are also group lessons at various levels for members and nonmembers. Enrollment is limited to six per class and tactics, techniques, fitness, and proper etiquette are covered. Private lessons are also offered, in one, six, and ten-lesson packages (call 212-875-4148 for squash information only).

92nd Street Y (212-996-1100)
1395 Lexington Avenue at 92nd Street

Four racquetball courts for members. Half-hour and hour-long private lessons, plus small group instruction are available.

TABLE TENNIS

THE EXACT ORIGINS OF THIS GAME ARE UNKNOWN, BUT IT WAS POPULAR HERE AND IN ENGLAND IN THE LATE 1800'S. They used a web-covered ball then and called the game either *whiff-whaff* or *gossima.* In 1902, however, the familiar celluloid ball and rubber-covered paddle were introduced. The game was then popularized under the name Ping Pong, the sound made as the ball hit the paddle, the table, and the other paddle. And if you know that "onomatopoeia" is the literary term for words that sound like what they're describing (like *buzz, crackle,* and *Ping Pong*), you should feel real good about yourself.

Playing

Amsterdam Billiard Club (212-570-4545)
210 East 85th Street between 2nd and 3rd Avenues
Three tables are available.

The Billiard Club (212-206-7665)
220 West 19th Street between 7th and 8th Avenues
Table tennis on the first floor and pool tables on the second floor.

Carmine Recreation Center (212-242-5228)
Clarkson Street and 7th Avenue South
One table is here.

Hackers, Hitters, & Hoops (212-929-7492)
123 West 18th Street between 6th and 7th Avenues
An interactive sports and entertainment bar with food, drink, and various sports activities. Three tables can be rented in increments of 15 minutes.

Le Q (212-995-8512)
36 East 12th Street between University Place and Broadway
Open 24 hours a day, there are two tables on the lower floor and 27 pool tables plus one billiards table on the first.

McBurney YMCA Y (212-741-9210)
215 West 23rd Street between 7th and 8th Avenues
Three tables are available at various times during the week.

West Side Billiards Club (212-246-1062)
601 West 50th Street (enter on 11th Avenue)
Eight tables (plus 13 pool tables). West Side runs a women's league on Sundays from October to February and provides year-round coaching and private lessons for men and women.

Leagues

Women Athletes of New York (212-759-4189)
The league runs from November to April and both individuals and teams are welcome. Matches take place in various Manhattan locations, and instruction is available.

TENNIS

If God had meant Wimbledon to be played in great weather, he would have put it in Acapulco. —AN ANONYMOUS BRITISH TENNIS OFFICIAL

THERE ARE 98 PUBLIC TENNIS COURTS IN MANHATTAN and another 387 scattered throughout the other boroughs. Happily, the courts in Manhattan are primarily located in parks or nearby water, so when you're playing like a barnyard animal, you can either take solace in some trees or throw yourself in a river. There are also numerous private clubs and countless schoolyard walls against which you can take out your forehand and backhand frustrations.

City Tennis

NYC Parks & Recreation Tennis Information (718-699-4200)

The season begins in early April and runs through November. There is also a winter season that starts in the beginning of December with play at various courts around town. A permit is required to play on city courts, and its cost depends on your age. Permits can be obtained both at the Arsenal (212-360-8131), located in Central Park at 5th Avenue and 64th Street, or at Paragon Sports (212-255-8036) at 18th Street and Broadway. Season permits go on sale at the end of March and are valid in all five boroughs. Without a permit, you can't make a court reservation in Central Park, and the waits can often be long. Single day passes are available for $5 and can be purchased at the Arsenal or at the Central Park Tennis Center.

City Courts

Central Park Tennis Center (212-280-0201) Mid-park on 96th Street

The Center has 26 Har-Tru and four hard courts and sponsors a number of tournaments. Clinics and lessons are offered by the eight teaching pros. There's a pro shop, snack bar, and locker room facilities (available for seasonal rental by permit holders. Permit holders can make reservations in-person or on the phone (Monday through Friday from noon to 2 PM, 212-280-0205). If you've never seen this place, it's definitely worth a visit.

East River Park Tennis (212-529-7185) Delancey Street and the FDR Drive (you must cross a bridge over the Drive)

The 12 outdoor hard courts are rarely as crowded as those in Central Park.

Riverside Park Tennis Courts (212-978-0277) Riverside Drive and 96th Street

Ten red-clay outdoor courts that can test your skill and patience (wind gusts coming off the Hudson have been known to make shots that would normally be in—very out. There are also ten hard courts further uptown at 119th Street and Riverside Avenue that are often not too crowded.

Inexpensive Instruction

Parks Department (212-360-1397)

They can arrange lessons from teaching pros at various city courts.

Riverbank State Park (212-694-3600)
Hudson River at 145th Street

Four outdoor hard courts that are open from the beginning of April to the end of November. Beginner classes are taught on in-season weekday evenings.

YWCA (212-755-2700)
610 Lexington Avenue at 53rd Street

Offers tennis instruction for beginners (forehand, backhand, service fundamentals) on their basketball court. There is a maximum of ten people per class, and if you don't have a racquet, they'll loan you one.

Clubs

Columbus Tennis (212-662-8367)
795 Columbus Avenue at 97th Street

Nine outdoor Har-Tru courts for members only, six of which are lit for night play. There are also individual, junior, family, and corporate options. Once a member, you'll have no additional fees for court time. Their season runs from early April to early November.

East River Tennis Club (718-937-2381)
44-02 Vernon Boulevard, at 44th Avenue, Long Island City

This facility has 18 Har-Tru outdoor courts (covered with a bubble in the winter), a pool, fabulous Manhattan views, and a shuttle bus from 57th Street and 3rd Avenue. A range of packages is available.

HRC Tennis (212-422-9300)
South Street, at the end of Wall Street

Eight Har-Tru courts in two air-conditioned bubbles, positioned lengthwise down the pier instead of side by side, which gives a feeling of privacy and space. HRC offers game arranging, lessons, free clinics, and tournaments. This is an enjoyable facility with comfortable locker rooms and well-maintained courts. There is an initiation fee to become a member, plus monthly dues and court time. Nonmembers can rent courts by the hour.

Manhattan Plaza Racquet Club (212-594-0554)
482 West 43rd Street at 10th Avenue

A first-class facility with five hard courts that are for members only. The courts are uncovered from May to September and under a bubble for the rest of the year. The club offers game arranging, clinics, private and group lessons, a weekend singles league (singles as in tennis, not as in looking for romance), a doubles clinic, and Friday night doubles parties. Members may reserve courts up to two weeks in advance. There is an initiation fee, membership dues, and hourly rates, which also get you access to a pro shop, lounge, locker room, saunas, sunbathing area and (for an extra charge) the health club's pool.

Midtown Tennis Club (212-989-8572)
341 8th Avenue at 27th Street

There aren't a lot of frills here, but the eight indoor Har-Tru courts are well-maintained (four are uncovered in the summer, and the other four remain under the bubble). The facility offers group and private lessons, Friday night tennis parties, summer Sunday leagues, singles challenge ladders, and doubles tournaments. Seasonal and hourly rates are available, and you can make reservations up to three weeks in advance.

National Tennis Center (718-760-6200) Flushing Meadow Park, Corona, Queens

Reservations can be made up to two days in advance on 24 outdoor courts (with lights for night play) and nine indoor courts. The facility is closed to the public at the end of August for two weeks for the U.S. Open. There are various rate schedules, and private lessons and group instruction are available.

Sutton East Tennis Club (212-751-3452) 488 East 60th Street at York Avenue, under the 59th Street Bridge

There are eight air-conditioned red-clay courts here along with—at no extra charge—the distant sound of trucks rumbling overhead. I used to play here and actually came to like the sound. You can reserve up to a week in advance, and group and private lessons are available. Sutton East also offers a match-up service, day and evening leagues, and round robin tournaments. Seasonal and hourly rates are available, the people at the desk are always friendly, and they keep the courts in great shape.

The Tennis Club at Grand Central (212-687-3841) 15 Vanderbilt Avenue, third floor of the terminal

There are two Decoturf courts here. If you really want to feel like you're getting away with something, book some time during a weekday morning or evening rush hour. While you're hitting your elegant backhand down the line for a winner, thousands of commuters are either rushing out of trains to get to work—or rushing into them to head home. There are hourly, seasonal, and yearly rates, and the courts are closed summer weekends.

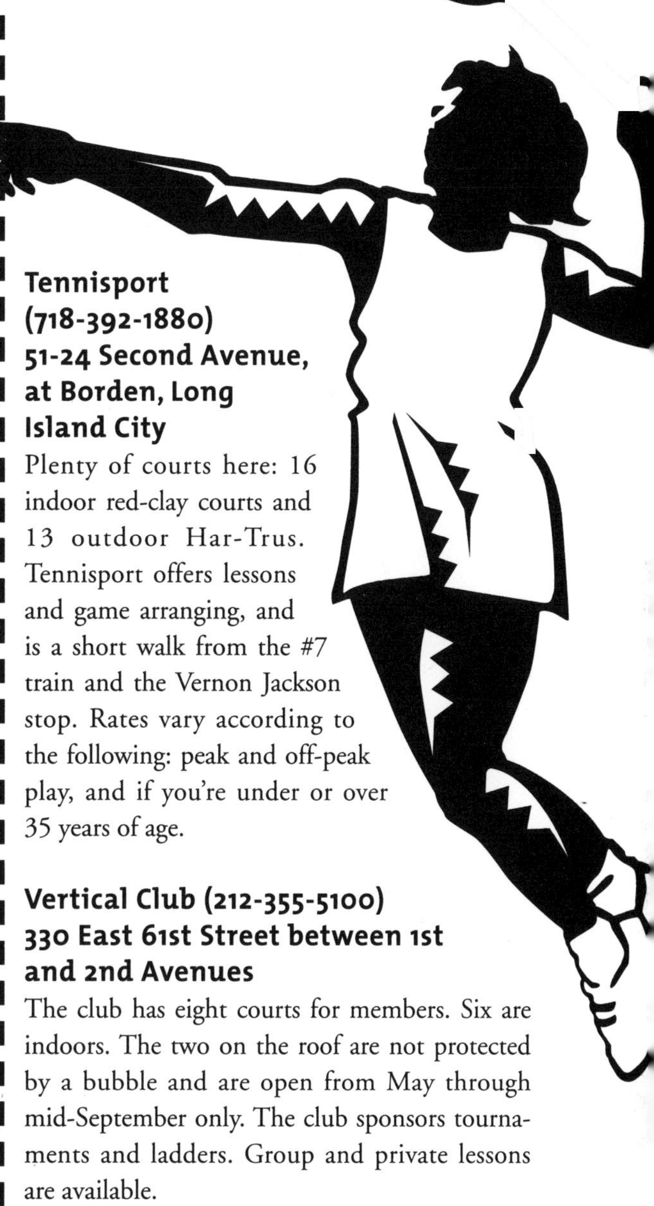

Tennisport (718-392-1880) 51-24 Second Avenue, at Borden, Long Island City

Plenty of courts here: 16 indoor red-clay courts and 13 outdoor Har-Trus. Tennisport offers lessons and game arranging, and is a short walk from the #7 train and the Vernon Jackson stop. Rates vary according to the following: peak and off-peak play, and if you're under or over 35 years of age.

Vertical Club (212-355-5100) 330 East 61st Street between 1st and 2nd Avenues

The club has eight courts for members. Six are indoors. The two on the roof are not protected by a bubble and are open from May through mid-September only. The club sponsors tournaments and ladders. Group and private lessons are available.

College Tennis

Columbia University (Manhattan) 212-854-2546
Fordham University (the Bronx) 718-817-4240
New York University (Manhattan) 212-998-2029
St. John's University (Queens) 718-990-6367
Wagner College (Staten Island) 718-390-3227

Surfing the Net

The U.S. Open
http://www.usopen.org/

The biggest tournament in the States runs from the end of August through the second week of September. Stay tuned to the website for current news, feature stories, player diaries, photos, information, the history of the tournament, and more.

Tennis Server
http://www.tennisserver.com/Tennis.html

This site will tell you everything there is to know about the sport: current news, equipment reports, training tips, rules, listings of clubs and organizations, and playing strategies. It also includes links to other tennis sites.

Did you know?

That on September 30, 1659 Governor Peter Stuyvesant forbade the playing of a tennis-like game during divine services? This is thought to be the first mention of the sport in the country.

That in the spring of 1894 Mary Ewing Outerbridge set up the first tennis court on the grounds of the Staten Island Cricket and Baseball Club, which went on to host the first important U.S. tournament?

10

SPORTS *on* the WATER

BOATING AND SAILING

I had a friend whose boyfriend insisted on taking her sailing. She said she didn't mind being terribly wet, or cold, or hungry, or seasick, or frightened. She just didn't like them all at once.

—DICK FRANCIS, English novelist

Boating

Loeb Boathouse
Central Park, near 74th Street and East Drive

There are nearly 200 rowboats available for use on the 18-acre lake, and the season runs from April through October. Evenings from May through the end of October, you and up to four friends can take a gondola ride on the 34' *Daughter of Venice*. The *Daughter* has been in this country since 1987 and continues a tradition that began when the park first opened when there was a restaurant at Bethesda fountain, and, for 20 years, two gondolas provided rides on the lake. For reservations call 212-517-2233.

Prospect Park (718-282-7789)
Prospect Park Lake, between Lincoln Road and Parkside Avenue

Pedal boats (not rowboats) are available for rent. The season runs from April to September.

Sundance (212-598-4726)
PO Box 40314, Brooklyn, NY 11240

Sundance is a nonprofit corporation that provides the gay and lesbian communities with a range of noncompetitive outdoor activities. In addition to boating, canoeing and rafting, they offer skating, biking, horseback riding (Western and English), skiing (downhill and cross-country), windsurfing, and hiking. Sundance organizes day trips, weekends, and week-long events, all of which are listed in their monthly newsletter.

Learning to Sail:

The Coast Guard Auxiliary (212-355-1564)

Gives free 15-week powerboat and sailing courses at Hunter College. Class usually begins in early February and ends in late May/early June (to take advantage of the start of boating season). There is also an advanced course in coastal navigation. A nominal fee is charged for books and materials.

Great Hudson Sailing Center (212-741-7245)
Chelsea Piers, West 23rd Street at the West Side Highway

The oldest nationally accredited sailing school on the river with a season that runs from April to October. Courses are offered in keelboat, coastal cruising, bareboat cruising, coastal navigation, and basic spinnaker.

Knickerbocker Sailing Association
PO Box 316, New York, NY 10011
http://www.geocities.com/WestHollywood/9543 • *reloren@ibm.net*

The association brings together men and women who love sailing and are comfortable in a gay environment. They have about 70 members and 20 boats. The Association hosts monthly meetings, arranges convoys, flotillas, and charters, and publishes a newsletter.

Manhattan Sailing School
(212-786-3323)
North Cove Marina at the World Financial Center

Offers a basic sailing course on J/24 sailboats with four students per class maximum and a money-back guarantee. You can take the course over a single weekend or during five weekday evenings. In addition to basic sailing, you can take classes in coastal cruising, bareboat chartering, and offshore passage making. And if you prefer private to group lessons, this can be arranged. The school also hosts a number of events in the harbor, has daily rentals and charters, and offers membership in the **Manhattan Yacht Club.** The club provides access to the school's fleet, participation in races and cruises, social events, and a discount on dockage for boat owners.

Newport Sailing School
(201-626-3210)
500 Washington Boulevard, Jersey City, NJ (10 minutes on the PATH train)

Winner of the American Sailing Association's annual Sailing School of the Year Award five times, the school limits their class size to three and offers a basic sailing course with two classroom sessions and four days on the water. All the instructors are ASA- and U.S. Sailing-certified, and the school sails J/24s. The school allows you to retake any course for free if not completely satisfied. Courses include basic sailing, advanced sailing, coastal cruising, bareboat charter preparation, introduction to racing, championship racing, and coastal navigation. They also run the **Newport Cruising Club,** which provides members access to their fleet of J/24 and J/30 sloops during a May 10 through October 26 season. And if you're interested in sailing the Caribbean, Newport conducts an annual Caribbean Cruising Flotilla.

New York Sailing School
(914-235-6052)
22 Pelham Road, New Rochelle, NY

Introductory and intensive sailing courses on Long Island Sound are taught on 23' Sonars (four students per boat), which the school considers to be the "best classroom afloat." The boats are also available for rent after you graduate. New York Sailing has been in business for 28 years and lets you take a course again for free if you're not completely satisfied. The school offers a learn to sail course, as well as classes in coastal cruising, coastal navigation, bareboat chartering, racing, and a spinnaker workshop. In addition, they host a wide variety of special events, regattas and alumni sails, and sunset cruises. A Passport Sailing Club membership allows for unlimited sailing.

Sailing on a (Much) Smaller Scale:

Kerbs Model Boathouse or Conservatory Water (212-360-8133) East 74th Street, off Fifth Avenue

You can give your model boat a workout here. Every Saturday from 10 AM to 2 PM, members of the Model Yacht Club of Central Park bring out their radio-controlled boats and have a miniature regatta. Smirk as much as you want, but some of these toys cost $1,000 and more. You can request a permit to store your boat.

Sailing the Net

Sailrace
http://www.sailrace.com/

This site is dedicated to sailing and racing in the New York area and offers current news, racing results, a sailing calendar, club and association listings, announcements, a bulletin board, and other sailing links.

Did you know?

That a boat race in New York harbor in 1824 attracted an estimated crowd of 50,000? The crew of the winning craft *Whitehall* won a $1000 prize and became civic heroes.

That the Castle Garden New York Amateur Boat Club Association was the first such association of its kind in the United States? It was founded in 1834 and was intended for "young men of the highest respectability, who were determined to combine pleasure with the utmost propriety of conduct."

CANOEING AND KAYAKING

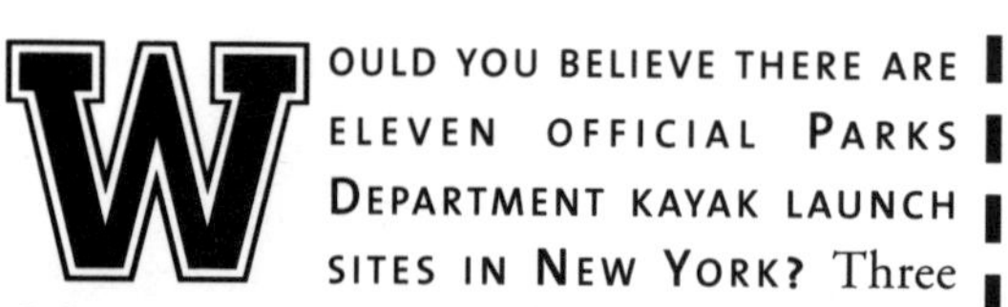

WOULD YOU BELIEVE THERE ARE ELEVEN OFFICIAL PARKS DEPARTMENT KAYAK LAUNCH SITES IN NEW YORK? Three of them are in Manhattan: the 79th Street Boat Basin, Riverside Park at 148th Street, and Inwood Hill Park at the foot of Dyckman Street. (Is this a great city, or what?) The kayaking season runs from April to November, and all you need is an inexpensive permit that's available at the Arsenal (212-360-8131) in Central Park at 5th Avenue and 64th Street.

Learning

Manhattan Kayaking Company (212-336-6068) Chelsea Piers, West 23rd Street at the West Side Highway

Conducts a kayaking program with group instruction that begins in their pool and then moves into the river between their piers. There are various levels of classes designed to help train the muscle groups needed for the sport, teach basic maneuvers, and ultimately get paddlers out on the river itself. They also have a kayak storage facility that holds some 25 boats. They also offer night paddles, trips, sunset tours, and more. One of the tours circles around the Statue of Liberty.

Outdoor Bound (212-505-1020)

In business for over 15 years, Outdoor Bound arranges one-day (about an hour's drive from town) and two- to six-day canoeing, kayaking, whitewater rafting, hiking, and cross-country skiing trips in New York State and throughout the Northeast. The price typically includes equipment rental, guides, lessons, transportation—and accommodations when appropriate. Call for their catalog which contains all their seasonal offerings and identifies levels of difficulty.

Randy Henriksen (212-924-1327) New York Kayak Company

Offers both group and private lessons with internationally known instructors and sells a full line of folding and hardshell kayaks, clothing, and accessories.

Riverbank State Park (212-694-3600) Hudson River at 145th Street

Offers a basic canoeing class on weekends.

Clubs

Appalachian Mountain Club (212-986-1430) http://www.outdoors.org

Hosts a regular series of canoe classes and trips, in addition to hiking and fishing excursions and more. The club is a conservation and recreation organization that has been in existence for over 100 years. It has about 72,000 members in 11 regional chapters and sponsors numerous events—most of which are planned for New Yorkers who typically don't own cars. There are yearly membership dues and many events are open to members and nonmembers alike.

The Downtown Boathouse (Jim Wetteroch at 212-966-1852) Pier 26, North Moore Street, five blocks south of Canal Street

The Boathouse is a nonprofit, all-volunteer outfit with its own launch site. They sponsor events, offer lessons, and have storage room for about 100 boats. They are open weekends and holidays, 9 AM to dusk, from April 15th to October 15th and hope to expand the hours and programs.

Metropolitan Canoe and Kayak Club (contact Ed Goufas at 201-437-3814 or Mel Silverman at 914-634-9466)

This club promotes safe and responsible kayaking and canoeing and sponsors paddling trips just about all year-round. There are many one-day and two-day trips (with overnight camping or motel stays). The organization hosts introductory and refresher paddling clinics open to members and nonmembers alike. The first clinic covers paddle selection, canoe handling, entering and debarking at a dock, basic self-rescue, and maneuvering in tandem. The second clinic covers solo paddling, slide slipping, sharp turns, beach landings, paddling in the wind, and rescue tactics. The club has a number of canoes and kayaks that members can rent, and annual dues also entitle you to a newsletter, *Metropolitan Paddler,* with articles and an extensive calendar of events.

Sebago Canoe Club (718-241-3683)
Paerdegat Basin, foot of Avenue N, Brooklyn, NY

Offers canoe and kayak trips, courses, and competitions, and publishes a very interesting newsletter.

Sierra Club (718-370-2096)
Box 880, Planetarium Station, New York, NY 10014

Sponsors a full schedule of year-round events for almost every interest and skill level. Membership dues are very affordable and get you a quarterly *Outings* schedule filled with canoeing, hiking, biking, and skiing events, and more. All the activities are fully explained, and the degree of difficulty is indicated. Since the people who run this chapter really have things together, there are also clear instructions about how to get where you're going by car or public transportation.

Did you know?
That the first canoe club in the United States was the New York Canoe Club, started on Staten Island in 1871?

FISHING

Fishing, with me, has always been an excuse to drink in the daytime.

—JIMMY CANNON, sportswriter

MY FRIEND RICHARD CALLED ONE DAY AND ASKED IF I WANTED TO GO FISHING. I said sure, but never expected what came next. Poles in hand, we walked to the subway at 72nd and Broadway, rode the express to Fulton street, strolled a few blocks to the South Street Seaport, and then stepped onto Captain Joe Shastay's boat *Mako* to fish for striped bass in New York harbor. Did we catch anything? Richard did, Joe did, but I didn't. But how about fishing 200 yards from the Statue of Liberty? Fishing directly under the Brooklyn Bridge? Fishing offshore from the United Nations and close to Ellis Island? Fishing until the sun begins to set over the Verrazano Bridge? And then how about having beer and fried clams at the Seaport and riding the subway home, accompanied by the sidelong glances of an incredulous rush-hour crowd? Great fun.

Fly Fishing in Central Park

You can fish in the lake by the Boathouse, in the 59th street pond, and in the Harlem Meer (110th Street near 5th Avenue), but fishing is prohibited in the Reservoir. (Can't you just imagine the size of all those bass, perch, and catfish who spend their lives eating, swimming, having babies, and laughing at us?) About 50 to 75 people fly fish regularly year-round, although the best fishing is from April to mid-June, and September, October, November. You'll need a New York State license from the Department of Environmental Conservation (718-482-4885). And you'll need to practice telling fish stories because you won't ever have proof of the eight-pounder you caught within sight of the Dakota. Everything is catch and release.

Harlem Meer
(212-860-1370)
110th Street near Fifth Avenue

Meer is a Dutch word meaning "small sea," and this one is an 11-acre lake stocked with some 50,000 largemouth bass, catfish, golden shiner, bluegill, and more. You can borrow poles and get bait at the Charles A. Dana Discovery Center, and you don't even need a license. Harlem Meer is an absolutely beautiful spot right at the northern end of Central Park. It has well-kept lawns, beautiful trees, large rocks, and walkways with benches. It also has a large population of geese and ducks, plus pigeons, swans, and a few seagulls. Many of these birds have become very accustomed to people, and, the last time I was there, three geese stood right in the middle of a path and wouldn't move out of my way. I came to within a few inches of them, and they still wouldn't move. Not only did they force me to walk around them, but they stared right at me all the way. Can swans smirk?

Fishing on the Hudson River

The Hudson River Conservancy
(212-533-PARK)
Pier 25, at North Moore Street, five blocks south of Canal Street

Sponsors catch and release fishing on the weekends. As they say in their flyer, "The Conservancy supplies the rods, reels, bait, and instruction, and the Hudson River supplies the fish." (For more information about the Hudson River Conservancy, see page 29.)

Fishing Boats

IN TOWN

Captain Joe Shastay
(201-239-1988)

You and two friends can meet Joe's 19' *Mako* at the South Street Seaport or East 23rd Street Marina for evening fishing from March to January in New York Harbor. Daytime and weekend trips can also be arranged. Fall fishing is usually for stripers, while in the summer it's stripers and blues. And if you've ever gone out on a party boat that seemed to cruise forever before getting to the fishing grounds, that's not the case with Joe. You'll have a line in the water in about ten to 15 minutes.

Rocket Sportfishing Charters (Captain Tony Dilernia, 718-423-6007)
This vessel sails from the East 23rd Street Marina and takes one to six people for after-work trips that run from 5:30 to 9:30 PM. Step aboard his custom-made *Rocket* in your business suit, change clothes below, and reemerge ready to fish. Morning (6 AM to 10 AM), mid-day (noon to 4 PM), or all-day (8 AM to 3 PM) trips can also be arranged. Included in the price is bait and tackle, and even your choice of food and drink. Tony is quick to point out that, outside of Chesapeake Bay, the Hudson River is the largest single producer of striped bass in the world, and every striper feeding or spawning there has to pass through New York Harbor. So it's stripers in season, and also blues, sea trout, fluke, and blackfish—all usually a half-hour away from the dock. Tony is a marine biologist by training and a professor at a local college with over twenty years of charter experience.

A Little Further Away

**Captain Carl (718-885-0236)
City Island**
Riptide lll goes out for blues and flukes starting at 8 AM every day from March 1st through December 15th.

***Pastime Princess* (718-252-4398)
Emmons & Bedford Streets, Sheepshead Bay, Brooklyn**
Offers half-day and evening trips in the summer, and all-day trips in the winter. A recorded telephone announcement lets you know the intended catch of the day.

***The Sea Queen II* (718-332-2423)
Emmons Avenue, Pier 6, Sheepshead Bay, Brooklyn**
Operates March 1st through Thanksgiving on the following schedule: Flounder begins March 1st, fluke on June 1st, and striped bass November 1st. Captain George Aswad runs half-day and full-day trips, New Moon striped bass trips, and an annual fluke derby. He also goes out on a 4th of July fireworks cruise.

A Little Further Still

**Captain Steve Jagoda (914-423-6464)
Mamaroneck, NY**
Takes one to five people on half-day and full-day trips to western Long Island Sound for bass, blues, flounder, and fluke. Steve provides bait and tackle and also has a smaller boat for fly fishermen.

**Captain Pete Peterson (914-738-4593)
New Rochelle, NY**
Klondike lX, which can accommodate about 120 fishermen, makes full-day trips for blues and stripers (8 AM to about 4:30 PM) from April to Thanksgiving. Bait and tackle are available onboard.

Farthest

You can fish your way, marina by marina, from New York City to the end of Long Island, but if you want to go far from home, you might as well go directly to Montauk, where dry land ends.

Viking Fleet (516-668-5700)
Runs three boats, so they probably have one that leaves when you want to go, and fishes for what you want to catch. The fleet has half-day, full-

day, evening trips, plus four-day fish-a-thons. They supply all bait and tackle, give free fishing lessons, and also coordinate whale watching cruises, fall foliage tours, and more.

Captain Bill Ricca (516-543-4529)
http://www.sportfishli.com/alyssa.htm
The *Alyssa Ann* takes one to six passengers inshore for bass, cod, blues, blackfish, and flounder, and offshore for tuna, shark, marlin, and dolphin. In addition, you can arrange a long-range wreck trip for giant summer cod, pollack, and hake. The *Alyssa Ann* has won numerous tournaments and landed Montauk's largest shark to date: 560 lbs. Bill's season usually runs from late March to mid-December.

Buying and Learning

Manhattan Custom Tackle
(212-505-6690)
913 Broadway between 20th and 21st Streets
Sells custom gear for both fly and surf fishing, as well as licenses. They are very knowledgeable about what's going on where.

The Urban Angler (212-979-7600)
118 East 25th Street between Park and Lexington Avenues
Dedicated to fly fishing, the Angler sells gear and licenses and offers lessons on fly tying for fresh and salt water, as well as how to cast. They can hook you up (no pun intended) with area guides.

A Club

Appalachian Mountain Club
(212-986-1430)
http://www.outdoors.org
In addition to hosting fishing trips, they arrange canoeing, hiking and assorted other excursions. (For more information about the Appalachian Mountain Club, see page 101).

And When You're in the Hamptons

and get the urge to fish, call David Blinken. David does business under the name of **North Flats Guiding** and teaches fly fishing, fly tying, and light tackle. He is also a guide, and fishes the waters between Sag Harbor and Montauk. David's season runs from mid-May through early December. You can reach him in-season at 516-324-3241 and off-season at 212-517-3474.

Surfing the Net

Sportfish Long Island
http://www.sportfishli.com/index.htm
Provides information for the Freeport to Montauk region about party and open boats, deep sea and surf fishing, and tournaments. Also has links to weather and other fishing-related sites.

Did you know?
That on September 4th, 1609, a crew from Henry Hudson's *Half Moon* cast a net from either Coney Island or Sandy Hook (the historical record is unclear) and caught "ten great mullets, of a foot and a halfe a peace, and a ray as great as foure men could hale into the ship"?

SURFING

SURFERS ARE SECRETIVE AND EXTREMELY DEVIOUS. They protect their special surfing spots like mama bears protect cubs, and "foodies" protect favorite restaurants. I remember how the Malibu Surfing Association would keep tourists and other surfers away by taking down the sign identifying Malibu Beach, and then reinstalling it a few miles up the road. The City of Los Angeles would put up a new sign, and the surfers would take it down and move it. The City would put up a new sign again, and the surfers would take it down again. Although they may be devious, the fact is there's no place for surfers to hide. When they're on the water, they're *on the water,* so my best advice for you surf seekers is to drive or walk the beaches mentioned below. If surfers are there, so's the surf.

Long Island Surfing Locations

Cedar Beach
Babylon, Long Island

Take the Long Island Railroad to the Babylon stop or, if driving, take the Long Island Expressway to Exit 51. You'll find surfers past Jones Beach near the Fire Island inlet.

Fire Island

For directions, call the Fire Island National Seashore, 516-289-4810. Once there, just look for surfers.

Gilgo Beach
Babylon, Long Island

Gilgo is a pickup of Cedar Beach in the town. See above for directions. Once there, just look for surfers.

Jones Beach
Wantagh, Long Island

There are various car, bus, and train options. Call 516-785-1500 for directions. Surf's up at the far west end.

Lido Beach
Hempstead, Long Island

You basically have to drive here. Call the Park at Lido Beach for directions, 516-431-6650. Just look for surfers when you get there.

Long Beach

Take the Long Beach Branch of the Long Island Railroad to the last stop. For driving instructions, call City Hall at 516-431-1000. Just look for surfers on the beach.

Montauk

Take the Long Island Railroad to various Hamptons stops, or, if driving take the Long Island Expressway to Exit 70 (the Hamptons). You'll find surfers at Montauk and throughout most of the Hamptons. At Westhampton Beach, try K Street.

Robert Moses State Park

Exit 53 off the Long Island Expressway. Surfers can generally be found around fields 3 and 4.

Rockaway Beach

Tom Sena of **Rockaway Beach Surf Shop** (718-474-9345) at Beach and 116th, has checked out the beach at least four times a day for something like 30 years, and nobody knows more about the surfing conditions than he does. He also sells used and new boards at prices that are hard to beat. The beach is accessible by subway. Call Tom for precise directions.

Did you know?

That evidence suggests the Incas surfed in and around what is now Peru?

That when missionaries arrived in Hawaii in the early 1820's, they took one look at surfing and immediately banned it as both immodest and a waste of time?

WHITEWATER RAFTING

I FIRST TRIED THIS SPORT UPSTATE IN THE HUDSON RIVER GORGE. It was late fall and bloody cold. A friend and I slept the night in a rustic cabin not far from the river, had a large breakfast the next morning, and arrived at the launch site with the temperature hovering in the low 30's. The river was *roaring* in our ears, looking as angry as it sounded. This no longer seemed like a very good idea.

We struggled into wetsuits and life vests, were briefed on how to paddle, and were then cautioned that if we went overboard, we should aim downstream feet-first to help avoid unpleasantries with underwater rocks. Then we pushed off. Six novices plus a guide.

This turned out to be one of the best sports experiences of my life: exciting, thrilling, and a little scary. We paddled together like we'd been doing it for years. The advice about going downstream feet-first came in handy because everyone went overboard. Everyone, that is, except for one guy. In fact, most of us went over two or three times, and it turned out to be fun. We were quickly pulled back in, sputtering and laughing, which added a great deal to the experience and the camaraderie. Except for this one guy. And I don't know who else this bothered, but it bothered me. Not only wasn't this guy in the spirit of things, but he was even smug about not going over. And as the trip started to wind down, his smugness became arrogance, and that really started to grate on me. You know what's coming, right?

Finally we were at a long, calm patch in sight of where we'd go ashore. So I took my paddle, placed it squarely in the middle of his chest, and pushed. He went overboard, hit the water with an immensely satisfying splash, surfaced, and was clearly not amused. Well, I was, and so were the rest of my boatmates. And you know, it's been a few years since this happened and I've had enough time to feel childish about it, but I don't.

(*Note:* Since the places listed below are fairly far away, and rafting can be exhausting, consider resting for a night before making the drive home.)

Rafting

Hudson River Rafting Company (800-888-RAFT)
North Creek, NY

Organizes rafting excursions on the Moose River, one of the most intense in the East, during the month of April. *BIG* Class 5 water, scary and thrilling—and best for people with at least Class 4 experience. And you have lots of other choices. They raft the Hudson River Gorge in the spring and the fall. Spring offers continuous world-class rapids, and fall features great foliage and a more relaxed experience. It's the Black River Canyon in spring, summer, and fall, with exciting water year-round due to a dam release schedule. You can also try the Sacandaga River during the same three seasons which has calm water that is suitable for families. As an alternative to rafts, they also provide tubing, canoes, and inflatable kayaks here. If you've never tried rafting before, tell the Hudson River people how frightened you'd like to be, and they'll tell you what size water will do the trick.

Kittatinny Canoes (800-356-2852)

Dingman's Ferry, PA (about 2-1/2 hours away)
Offers whitewater rafting on the Delaware. Depending on river and weather conditions, they're open from mid-April through October. The Delaware is a National Scenic and Recreational river protected by the National Park Service, and you'll find that it and the surrounding woods are very beautiful. If you fall in love with the area, you can also canoe with Kittatinny, as well as kayak, camp, and take foliage tours in the fall and wildflower and wildlife tours in the summer. They also have ten paintball fields up in the mountains, so if you've always wanted to combine the chaos of the rapids with the chaos of paintball, you can do it here.

Whitewater Challengers (800-443-8554)
White Haven, PA

These folks have been guiding rafting trips for over 20 years. In New York State they raft the Hudson River Gorge, Black River Canyon, and the middle, lower, and bottom Moose River. In Pennsylvania they lead trips to the Lehigh River, which can also include biking excursions (from 10 to 25 miles along the river), whitewater kayak clinics (a two-day course for beginners), overnight camping (with various food options), and an interesting range of rafting/biking, eating/sleeping combinations. It takes approximately 2-1/2 hours to drive to their Lehigh River site.

And if You Want to Go Further

Zoar Outdoors (800-532-7483)
Charelmont, MA (about 3-1/2 hours away)

Choose to whitewater in Massachusetts or in Vermont. Plus, learn to kayak or canoe—and then do river runs in either. Kayak and canoe trips, and rock climbing instruction are also available.

Moxie Outdoor Adventures (800-866-6943)
You can raft in Maine on the Kennebec, Dead, and Penobscot Rivers, or choose to be closer to home on the West River in Vermont, The Deerfield in Massachusetts, or the Bull's Bridge Gorge in Connecticut. If you're going to Maine, it's over eight hours away, so you might want to consider Moxie's on-site cabins, platform tents, or campsites.

WIND SURFING

THERE IS A BEACH IN MAJORCA THAT DRAWS WIND SURFERS FROM JUST ABOUT EVERYWHERE IN THE WORLD. The winds seem to howl all the time, and the sight of hundreds of sails, boards, and riders on the water is spectacular—a riot of colors and speed and excited whoops in multiple languages that drift ashore in bits and snatches as the wind shifts. If you can't make it to Spain this weekend, however, maybe you can go somewhere on Long Island instead:

Belleview Park Center Moriches
There is free parking year-round, and you'll need to be careful of heavy summer boat traffic in the channel.

Hart's Cove
East Moriches Coast Guard Station
Parking is free year-round, but you'll have to fight jet skis on the best days.

Shore Road
Remsenburg
Free parking year-round, and lots of summer boat traffic in the channel.

West Meadow Beach
Stony Brook
Free parking year-round, and on great afternoons there's usually 20 or more boards on the water.

Napeague Harbor
Between Napeague and Montauk (Turn off Montauk Highway at the Art Barge.)
The best sailing here is at the northern end, where it's too shallow for boats. Without an East Hampton permit, however, parking can be a problem.

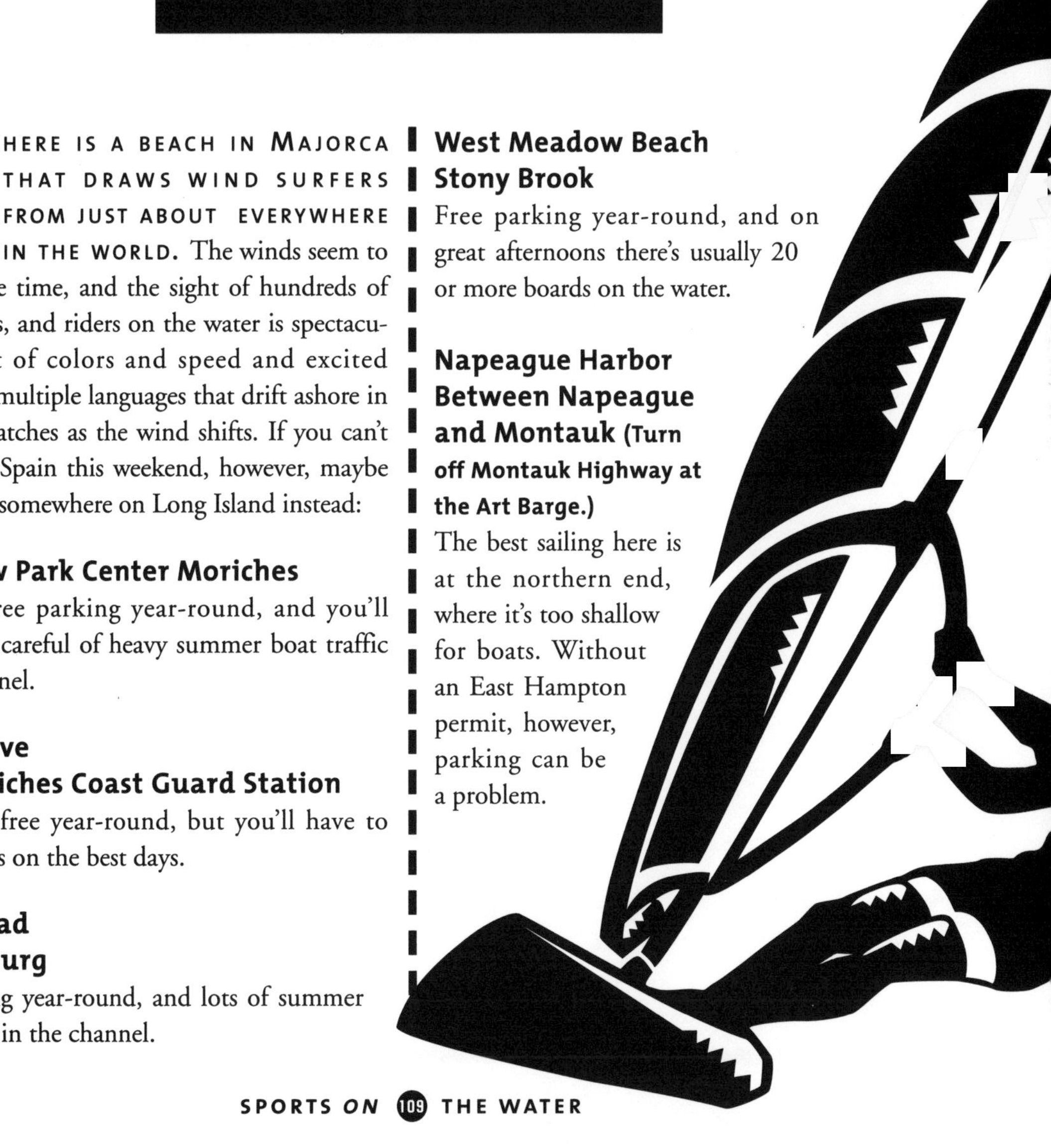

Learning and Renting

Main Beach Water Sports
(800-SPORT61 or 516-287-0828)
35 Shrubland Road, Southampton

Offers private and group windsurfing lessons, including equipment. Lessons are held on a private beach in an inlet of Peconic Bay. There's free parking, picnic facilities, drinks and snacks, and an on-site bathroom and changing room. If you're going to spend regular time in the Hamptons, you can buy a season pass to use any piece of equipment you need (so as you get better, you can progress from beginner boards to intermediate and advanced). If you feel more comfortable with a paddle in your hands, Main Beach also rents kayaks and canoes.

Windsurfing Hamptons
(516-283-9463)
1686 North Highway (Route 27), Southampton

A full-service windsurfing shop that offers rentals and lessons on Peconic Bay. The shop prefers one-on-one instruction, but will do groups of up to four if pressed. And although it's not in writing anywhere, they just about *guarantee* that you'll be up and sailing during your first lesson. The head instructor here is Jace Panebianco, who's on the pro circuit.

11

SPORTS *in the* WATER

DIVING

I DON'T KNOW WHY I'M NOT A BIGGER FAN OF DIVING; my only underwater experience was fabulous. It took place about a half hour away from Cancun, in a very popular park and beach called Xel-Ha (pronounced shell-ha). In season, the place is crowded with tourists and local families who swim and picnic around a large bay, and snorkel off a special dock. My wife and daughter wanted to try, so I went along. I rented gear, slipped into the water, and instantly found myself eye-to-eye with every tropical fish I've ever ooohed and aaahed about. There were iridescent green and red and blue ones, others with stripes, dots, and random splashes of color, and still others that looked like they were wearing lipstick.

Learning to Scuba Dive

Aqua-Lung School of New York (212-582-2800)

Around since 1964, this school offers a basic course over eight evenings. The school offers very flexible schedules. You can come once or twice a week, and even miss a class (picking up where you left off the next time). The training allows you to progress at your own speed, and you can take extra classes if you need them at no charge. The school provides all the equipment, including masks, fins, and snorkel. You need to make three open-water dives for basic international certification, which can either be done through the school when the weather is warm, or on your own during the winter. Advanced training is also available for those interested in dive master or instructor levels.

Asphalt Green (212-369-8890, Ext. 225) 555 East 90th Street at York Avenue

Offers group sessions throughout the year that combine classroom work, pool work, and open water dives. You need to supply your own fins and mask, and you can arrange to have private rather than group lessons.

Sea Horse Divers (212-517-2055)

Offers a platinum private and semiprivate dive course that can be completed in one week. It consists of three one-hour pool sessions and a weekend morning or weekday evening of class work. Their gold course is a group program designed for completion in three weeks. Four open-water dives are required for certification, and Sea Horse usually does this on-site in Pennsylvania. (The fee includes sleeping accommodations and equipment as well.)

West Side Y (212-787-4400) 5 West 63rd Street between Central Park West and Broadway

Conducts scuba classes in the pool three or four evenings a week.

Learning and Taking Trips

Pan Aqua Diving (212-736-3483)

In business for over 15 years, they have a 19-hour classroom and pool course, with additional no-charge hours provided as needed. Pan Aqua conducts training during the week and on weekends at East and West Side locations, and offers a free "try scuba night" (call for details). Pan Aqua also offers open water dives from New Rochelle (a short distance by car or Metro North), and a full range of dive trips and vacations to such locations as the Grand Caymans, Cozumel, the Galapagos, Honduras, Bequia, Turks & Caicos, Tortola, Nassau, Australia, and New Guinea.

SWIMMING

It only hurt once, from beginning to end. —JAMES COUNSILMAN, on swimming the English Channel at the age of 58

THE CITY OPERATES 33 OUTDOOR POOLS, 12 of which are in Manhattan, and only open during July and August. Usually very crowded and kid-intensive, memberships and entry fees, however are cheap.

City Pools

Asser Levy Recreation Center
(212-447-2020)
East 23rd Street and the FDR Drive

Built in 1906 as a public bathhouse and modelled on Roman baths, the center has a marble lobby, 20' ceilings, and was completely renovated in 1990. The outdoor pool measures 126' x 50' (with no lap lanes) and the indoor pool 63' x 64' with three lanes (and skylights). The indoor pool is open from September through the end of June, and the outdoor pool is open from July 3rd through September 1st. Scheduled lap swimming is offered, as well as free swimming and instruction at various levels. This, like all the other city pools, can become crowded, but it's a good facility.

Carmine Recreation Center
(212-242-5228)
Clarkson Street and 7th Avenue South

Carmine has a 60' x 34' indoor pool with three lanes (not in great shape) that's open September to June, and a much larger, much nicer 100' x 75' outdoor pool that's open July and August. This is a real *neighborhood* pool, with lots of kids and families on weekends. Swimming instruction is available. DeNiro's pool scene from Scorsese's *Raging Bull* was shot here.

Hamilton Fish Recreation Center
(212-387-7687)
128 Pitt Street at Houston

These two outdoor pools rank at the top of the city facilities. One is reserved exclusively for adults. The season runs from July 4th through Labor day.

Semiprivate Pools

Asphalt Green AquaCenter (212-369-8890)
555 East 90th Street at York Avenue

There's little question that this is the premier swimming facility in the metropolitan area. The AquaCenter is a state-of-the-art, $24 million, 74,000 square foot complex with a wonderful feeling of light and space. There is a 50 meter Olympic-standard pool with wave-reducing gutter systems, wave-absorbing lane lines, touchpad timing systems, an underwater observation window, underwater sound system, diving boards, and moveable bulkheads. The last time I was there, they had moved the bulkheads around and had *16* lanes in use. So if you're a really *serious* swimmer, this is the place for you. Or, if you just want a terrific place to paddle around, this is still the place for you. There is also a snack bar, and a pro shop that carries goggles and masks, suits, T-shirts, bags, and more.

The AquaCenter offers a wide variety of programs. In fact, the choices fill four 8-1/2" by-11" catalog pages. Group, semiprivate, and private swimming lessons are offered for all levels, in addition to life guard training, water exercise, swimming clinics (faster freestyle, flip turns, better backstroke, how to butterfly), diving, and so on. The center even has a masters swim team. There are daily drop-in fees and various membership plans, depending on the programs and facilities you want to take advantage of trying.

Chelsea Piers (212-336-6000)
West 23rd Street at the West Side Hwy

The 75' x 45' pool with six lap lanes and windows lets in so much light it almost feels like you're swimming outside. Chelsea offers private, semiprivate, and group instruction for every ability level. After your swim, you can walk right onto a 6,000 square-foot sundeck to catch some rays and watch the river roll by. This is a beautiful facility.

McBurney YMCA (212-741-9210)
215 West 23rd Street between 7th and 8th Avenues

A 48' x 20' pool with six lanes and a full schedule of open swims, classes, and instruction. (*Historical note:* it's said that Merrill met Lynch here.)

92nd Street Y (212-996-1100)
1395 Lexington Avenue at 92nd Street

A 75' x 36' pool with four lap lanes and a wide variety of classes for beginners, advanced beginners, intermediates, and masters (competitive swimming, actually), and even classes for people with a fear of water. Private lessons and lifeguard training are available, as is a full schedule of lap and free swims.

Riverbank State Park (212-694-3600)
On the Hudson River at 145th Street

Riverbank has an 80' x 36' outdoor pool that's open in the summer months, in addition to an

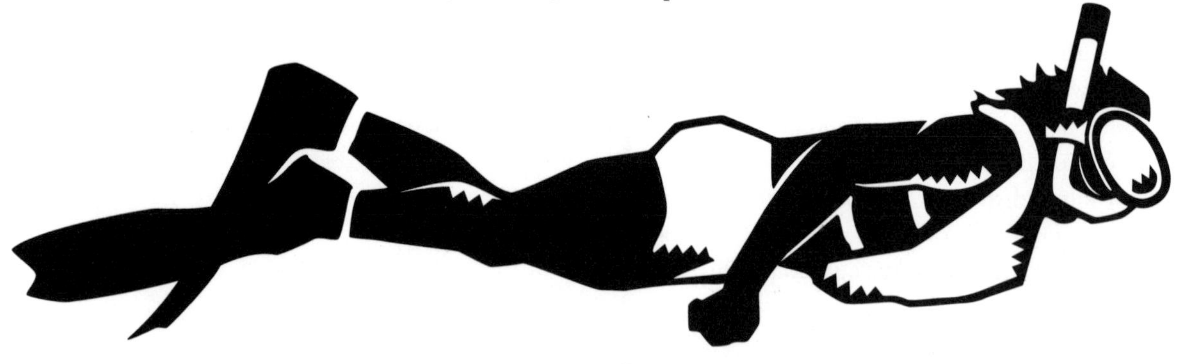

eight-lane 50-meter indoor pool with windows that open onto the river. There are early morning, afternoon, and evening lap swims, classes in stroke mechanics, three levels of beginning swimming, and two levels of advanced swimming. Also, there are Red Cross aquatic certification courses (CPR, Standard First Aid, Lifeguard Training). Riverbank is another beautiful facility.

Sheraton Manhattan Hotel Health Club (212-581-3300)

790 Seventh Avenue at 52nd Street

You can pay a drop-in fee to swim in this attractive, glass-enclosed 50' x 25' pool with four lanes. There's also a surrounding sundeck.

Vanderbilt YMCA (212-756-9600) 224 East 47th Street between 2nd and 3rd Avenues

There are two pools here: one (60' x 20') is used for classes, and the other (75' x 40' with six lanes) for laps. Vanderbilt offers a wide variety of programs, plus group and private instruction for beginners, intermediates, and advanced. This is an excellent facility with a friendly staff.

West Side Y (212-787-4400) 5 West 63rd Street between Central Park West and Broadway

The 45' x 20' pool is used primarily for lessons, and the 75' x 25' pool with four lanes is used almost exclusively for laps. Like most of the other Y's in the city, the West Side Y offers a wide variety of programs and instruction. You can join 12-session group classes in beginner, advanced beginner, or intermediate swimming, or arrange for private, one-on-one instruction.

YWCA (212-755-2700) 610 Lexington Avenue at 53rd Street

This *YWCA* is just as coed as all the *YMCAs* are, and it has two pools: a 45' training pool and a 75'x 36' general swim pool with six lap lanes. Seven levels of instruction are offered: from nonswimmers at Level 1 to people who want to refine *all* the strokes at Level 7. In addition, lifeguard and water-safety training programs are taught. You can either join on a yearly basis or pay a daily drop-in fee. Due to its mid-town location, this Y is actually busier on weekdays after work than on weekends.

Private Pools

Club La Raquette (212-245-1144) Parker Meridien Hotel, 119 West 56th Street, between 6th and 7th Avenues

Although day passes are available, this pool is really for club members and their guests (and for guests of the hotel). The glass-enclosed pool is in the hotel's penthouse and features lovely skyline and Central Park views. It is 40' x 20' and has up to four lap lanes. Instruction is available. (For more information about Club La Raquette, see page 90).

Manhattan Plaza Health Club (212-563-7001) 482 West 43rd Street at 10th Avenue

The 75' pool is situated in the atrium, surrounded by tropical plants and a sundeck, and is for the use of members and their guests. This may be the only place in town to offer a class in synchronized swimming. As long as you know the breast stroke, side stroke, back stroke, and crawl—you can sign up.

New York Health & Racquet Club 115 East 57th Street at Park Avenue (212-826-9650)

This location has a 40' x 20' pool with five lap lanes.

39 Whitehall Street between Pearl and Water Street (212-422-4653)
This location has a longer pool (60' X 20') but only two lap lanes.

NYHRC pools are open to members and their guests. Time is set aside for free and lap swimming, and instruction is available.

New York Sports Club
1637 3rd Avenue, at 91st Street (212-987-7200)
Has a 50' x 25' pool with six lap lanes.

1601 Broadway, at 49th Street (212-977-8880)
Has a 50' x 18' pool with four lap lanes.
Both are open to members and their guests, with time set aside for free and lap swimming. Instruction is available.

Reebok (212-362-6800)
160 Columbus Avenue between 67th and 68th Streets
They have a 75' pool with three lap lanes, plus a sauna, whirlpool, and sun deck. Instruction is available.

Instruction

Doug Stern (212-222-0720)
Runs swim clinics in the pool at Columbia Grammar School, 5 West 93rd Street. The Level 1 clinic covers stroke technique and conditioning; Level 2 covers conditioning and stroke review; Level 3 is "Different Stokes for Different Folks" and Level 4 is reserved for beginners who want to learn to swim and/or overcome a fear of water. Doug also teaches deep water running classes at John Jay College, which provide great nonimpact workouts.

A Club

Team New York Aquatics (212-691-3440)
A lesbian and gay masters swim team with about 200 members that works out eight times a week at John Jay and City College. All workouts are coached, and the lanes are divided by ability level so that everyone is challenged. The team participates in various local and national competitions, and welcomes fitness and competitive swimmers at every level.

Want to Swim 2.8 Miles in the River?

Then call The Hudson River Conservancy (212-533-PARK) about their annual Great Hudson River Swim. This swim is "with the tide," starts in the 79th Street Marina and ends at Pier 62—about an hour total. (For more information about the Conservancy, see pages 29, 103.)

You Say 2.8 Miles is Wimpy and You Want to Swim Around the Entire Island?

Manhattan Island Marathon Swim (888-NYCSWIM)
http://www.swimnyc.org
OK, then you can join the Annual Manhattan Island Marathon Swim. This is 28.5 miles of treacherous currents and strong tides, and it takes *very, very* good swimmers six to ten hours to complete the course.

College Swim Teams

Columbia University (Manhattan)
212-854-2546
St. John's University (Queens)
718-990-6367

Did you know?
That in 1877, the first U.S. championship swimming race was organized by the New York Athletic Club? It was one-mile long and was won by R. Weisenboth in 44 minutes, 44 seconds, and some odd hundredths.

WATER POLO

That's what I get for kicking Sans in his face. —Water polo player MIKE EVANS after he was ejected for kicking Spain's Jordi Sans.

THE "POLO" PART OF WATER POLO COMES FROM AN EARLIER VERSION OF THE GAME where players rode on barrels painted to look like horses, and hit at a ball with mallets. Happily, the modern version of the game looks far less foolish. I especially like the current feature that allows an opposing player to be held underwater. The rule book calls this "ducking." I might be more inclined to call it drowning.

Playing

Asphalt Green (212-369-8890)
555 East 90th Street at York Avenue
This coed program focuses on developing skills, but also includes scrimmages and competitions. Various membership plans are available.

YWCA (212-755-2700)
610 Lexington Avenue at 53rd Street
Frequently runs a coed water-polo league, beginning in early September with games on weekday evenings.

Playing on Inner Tubes

Chelsea Piers
(212-336-6000)
West 23rd Street at the West Side Hwy

Although inner-tube water polo isn't very macho, it's a lot of fun.

A Club

New York Athletic Club
(212-767-7000)
180 Central Park South at 59th Street and Seventh Avenue

They play serious water polo here. To join the NYAC you have to be sponsored by a current member, have two others endorse your application, and meet with someone from the membership board.

Team New York Aquatics
(212-691-3440)

Sponsors a lesbian and gay water polo team that works out at City College. The team scrimmages with local and regional teams and has about 20 active members. All ability levels are welcome and if you know how to swim, they will teach you the rest.

College Water Polo

Fordham University (the Bronx) 718-817-4240

Surfing the Net

United States Water Polo, Inc.
http://www.ewpra.org/uswp

Read about water polo teams, programs, clubs, and what's happening in the men's, women's, junior's, and masters' divisions. Plus, there's a calendar of events and links to other water polo sites.

12

SPORTS on WHEELS

BICYCLING

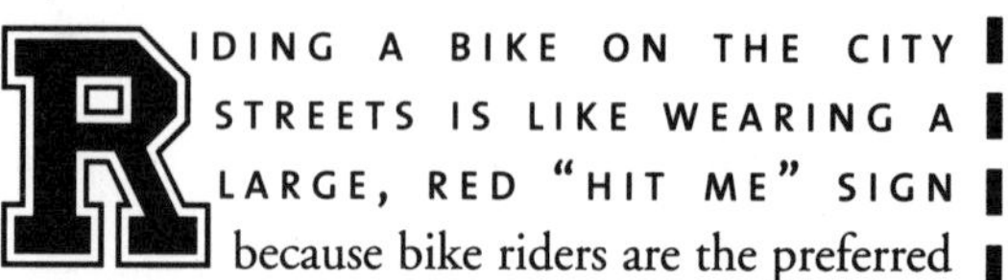

RIDING A BIKE ON THE CITY STREETS IS LIKE WEARING A LARGE, RED "HIT ME" SIGN because bike riders are the preferred target of cabs, fire engines, cars, buses, motorcycles, ambulances, vans, police cars, trucks, and 4-wheel drive recreational vehicles. Recent statistics tell the story: 5,193 crashes, 5,172 injuries, and 20 fatalities. Bicycling may be one of the most efficient and pleasant ways to get around town, but it's much safer to ride in the parks where you only have to worry about other cyclists, in-line skaters, and joggers.

Learning to Ride

Terry Chin (718-680-5227)

Offers private and group classes in Central Park. The private classes run about two hours and are long enough to get all but the most severely balance-challenged up and riding. Once a month in the park, Terry also teaches four-hour bike repair classes. Naturally, he sells a basic repair kit.

Learning to Race

Asphalt Green (212-369-8890)
555 East 90th Street at York Avenue

Bike racing is taught in a series of fifteen classes which meet in Central Park and cover pedaling, pack riding, climbing, sprinting, and racing dynamics. Each class combines a structured workout with interval work and race simulations. Participants are divided into groups by ability. A racing bike and approved helmet are required.

Clubs

Century Road Club Association (212-222-8062)

Nearly a hundred years old, this is the largest road racing club in the country. Members-only races are held on most Saturdays from March to November, and about four open races are also sponsored each year. The association also offers weekly training rides and serious instruction. Annual dues get you coaching, a newsletter, and discounts at selected bike shops.

Five Borough Bicycling Club (212-932-2300, ext. 350)

A nonprofit affiliate of American Youth Hostels, the club offers bike tours, sponsors races, and conducts bicycle repair courses. Annual dues entitle you to a bimonthly newsletter and information about all the club's activities.

New York Cycle Club (212-886-4545)

Around since 1979, the club sponsors rides around the city that depart from the Boathouse in Central Park. Other programming includes: weekend day rides, longer trips, and a 12-week workshop on bike care and repair. Members receive a monthly bulletin that lists all the club's activities and posts invitations to club-sponsored events.

Sierra Club (718-370-2096)

The Sierra Club has a full schedule of year-round bicycling events for almost every interest and skill level. (For more information about the Sierra Club, see page 102.)

Sundance (212-598-4726)
PO Box 40314, Brooklyn, NY 11240
Bicycling is just one of many activities sponsored by this nonprofit corporation devoted to the gay and lesbian communities. (For more information about Sundance, see page 98.)

Riding

Bite of Apple Tours (212-541-8759)

Offers a leisurely two-hour ride through Central Park with stops at all the major sights. A tour escort and bike rental are included in the price. Three tours (in English and in Spanish) are run daily (10 AM, 1 PM, and 5 PM), and each leaves from the NYC Visitors and Convention Bureau (2 Columbus Circle, at 59th Street).

Brooks' Country Cycling & Hiking Tours (212-874-5151)

Sponsors day trips to Connecticut, New Jersey, Long Island, Rhinebeck, and Bucks County; weekend trips to the Berkshires, Vermont, Cape May, and Shelter Island; and vacations around the country and in Europe. All the tours are rated either easy, moderate, or more difficult. Rental equipment is available.

The Great Five Boro Bike Tour

Typically held in May, this is the largest bicycling event in the country. It is a relatively flat and comparatively easy 42-mile ride through all five boroughs, and it concludes with a festival on Staten Island. The registration fee is $30. For more information, call Hostelling International-American Youth Hostels at 212-932-BIKE.

Transportation Alternatives (212-629-3311)

Runs the country's largest bicycling advocacy group, working to improve conditions for cyclists throughout the city. They also sponsor tours and races, and are a good source of information for most everything to do with the sport.

Transporting Bikes

Bikes are allowed on buses and subways, but be prepared for withering looks if you actually try to take one with you. And during rush hour, well, you'd really have to be desperate. Call the appropriate transit organization (PATH, LIRR, New Jersey Transit, the Staten Island Ferry) to find out about their rules and restrictions. You can buy a $6 Metro North Lifetime Bicycle pass at the Grand Central Customer Service window. This lets you take a bike on the train for free when you purchase a regular ticket.

City Cyclist

This free magazine that lists all the local bicycling events can be picked up at almost any bike shop.

Did you Know?

That in the mid-1800's, the new sport of *velocipeding* gained great popularity here? Schools for both sexes and all ages sprung up, and *Harper's Weekly* wrote, "Youngsters ride down Fifth Avenue with their schoolbooks strapped in front of their velocipedes, and expert riders cause crowds of spectators to visit public squares, which offer excellent tracks for the light vehicles to move swiftly over."

That when bikes first began to appear in Central Park, they were only permitted from midnight to 9 am?

That in May of 1880, the League of American Wheelmen (some 360-strong) held their annual meet in Central Park?

IN-LINE SKATING (AND ROLLER)

OLLER SKATES WERE APPARENTLY INVENTED AS AN ACT OF LOVE by Joseph Merlin. Merlin was a Belgian ice skating fanatic, who, in the 1760's, attached wheels to the bottom of his skates after all the ice melted so he could skate year-round. Of course nowadays, roller skates have been made virtually extinct by their successor, in-line skates, which are lighter, faster, smoother, and much more expensive.

Learning to Skate

Asphalt Green (212-369-8890)
555 East 90th Street at York Avenue

Has basic classes for balance, striding, stopping, turning, hill skating, and street awareness. Intermediate and advanced classes teach backwards skating, crossover, speed skating, advanced stopping, and freestyle. Rentals are available.

The Central Park Skate Patrol Skate School (212-439-1234)

Offers weekend beginner, intermediate, and advanced-level classes in in-line skating that meet outside Blades West, (120 West 72nd Street, between Broadway and Columbus). Each 75-minute lass is limited to 12 students. Helmets and wrist guards are required, and knee and elbow pads are strongly recommended. All the instructors are certified by the International In-line Skating Association. The Skate Patrol is probably best known for providing general assistance to users of Central Park and giving free stopping lessons to beginning skaters. They're the folks in the red T-shirts with the white crosses at the East and West 72nd Street entrances.

The Hudson River Conservancy (212-533-PARK)
Pier 25, at North Moore Street, five blocks south of Canal

Teaches in-line skating basics (how to stop, safety equipment, rules of the road) on Sunday afternoons. (For more information about the Hudson River Conservancy, see pages 29, 103, 116.)

New York Skateout (212-486-1919)

Offers group and individual beginner, intermediate, and advanced instruction with the emphasis on fitness, safety, and fun. In addition, they sponsor skate tours of Central Park (including a 45-minute loop at lunch) and cardiovascular skate workouts (progressive and nonimpact). They also organize TeamSkate, a social skating group that participates in civic activities, hosts brunches and special events, and skates together at least once a week.

92nd Street Y (212-996-1100)
1395 Lexington Avenue at 92nd Street

Presents in-line skating classes on weekday evenings with author and teacher Joel Rappelfeld and his Roll America staff. In Level 1, you learn balance, stopping, turning, hills, safety, and street awareness. In Level 2, it's backwards skating, crossovers, advanced stopping, speed, and artistic techniques. You can rent skates for the classes.

Skating

Battery Park City

There's great skating all around here, but you sometimes have to dodge a security guard who'd rather you were wheel-less.

Central Park

The most popular skating location in the city. On weekends you can skate the six-mile outer loop, the four-mile cutoff loop (which crosses the service road at 102nd Street), and the one-mile lower loop at anytime, but only when the park is closed to traffic during the week. You can also skate the bandshell (mid-park on 72nd Street) anytime. It's a good idea to bike or walk the cut-off loops before skating them for the first time so you'll know what to expect.

Chelsea Piers (212-336-6200)
West 23rd Street at the West Side Highway

Two large open-air concrete roller rinks with general skating, rentals, and lessons.

Hudson River Park Bikeway

Begins at Chambers Street and the river and stretches to 30th Street and eventually will continue to 59th Street.

Riverbank State Park (212-694-3600)
On the Hudson River at 145th Street

The 200' x 85' covered rink is used for roller skating in the summer and ice skating in the winter. Lots of families and children congregate here on weekends.

Riverside Park

There are two skate-friendly promenades along the river. The first runs from 72nd Street to about 83rd, and the other from 93rd to about 106th. Yes, you're right, they are crying out for a paved connection, which is said to be in the works.

Tompkins Square Park
East 7th to 10th Streets between Avenues A and B

This park has terrific surfaces, so if you're there when it isn't clogged with nonskaters, you can have a wonderful time. The basketball court in the park is where the National In-line Basketball League (see page 22) plays its games, so you know *that* surface has to be great.

Union Square
East 14th to 17th Streets, between Broadway and Park Avenue South

A fun place to skate when the Green Market isn't there. "No skating" signs are sometimes posted and sometimes not, and sometimes enforced and sometimes not.

Wall Street

Practically deserted on the weekends and lots of fun. Just you and all that money.

Wollman Rink (212-396-1010) Mid-Central Park at about 62nd Street

Roller and in-line skating take over from April to October.

Roller Disco: Outdoors

On balmy weekends, go midway into Central Park at about 72nd Street until you approach the Bandshell. Then listen for music. You will be beckoned to an area called the "Dead Road," where the Central Park Dance Skaters— experts and novices alike, are doing their thing. The music booms, and everyone boogies. It's a weekend-long party that you're free to join; just wait for a break in the circle and slide on in. And be sure to look for the guy on roller skates who goes round and round with a water bottle balanced on his head.

Roller Disco: Indoors

Roxy (212-645-5156) 515 West 18th Street between 10th and 11th Avenues

Roller disco two nights a week (one night's gay and the other's straight). Since the Roxy keeps changing the skating schedule, call for current days and times.

Trick Skating

There's a slalom course on the hill near Tavern on the Green (West Drive at 67th Street), created with 30 orange rubber cones, which regulars negotiate with amazing skill and speed: some frontwards and others backwards, some on two legs, others on one. If you're not too intimidated, go ahead and try it. But remember: Etiquette mandates that you replace all the cones you knock over. If this is too intense, go over to the Bandshell. There's a similar slalom course there, but it's on a flat patch. It's where people practice their forward and backward moves and their one- and two-legged passes. When they feel they're ready, they give the big course a try. Think of this as the Tavern's minor league.

Clubs and Just Bopping Around

Blade Night Manhattan (212-794-8513)

Every Wednesday night at 9 PM, bladers meet on the 14th Street steps of Union Square Park and begin an eight-mile, 90-minute jaunt through the streets of Manhattan. They follow a route that passes Grand Central, Rockefeller Center, the Central Park Bandshell, Tavern on the Green, Times Square, Madison Square Garden, Washington Square Park, St. Marks Place, and Battery Park. This skate is held in spring, summer, and fall, and ends about mid-December. It draws just a handful of hardy souls in the cold, but a few hundred can show up on beautiful spring and summer evenings. The crowd is mostly young, mostly single, mostly friendly. Get it?

The Central Park Moonlight Ride (212-802-8222)

Held on the last Friday of the month, with skaters meeting at 10 PM at the park entrance at Columbus Circle. This is a slow-paced, low-key affair, and you're encouraged to bring illumination to avoid unscheduled and unpleasant meetings with trees.

Empire Skate Club of New York (212-592-EMPIRE) http://www.skatecity.com/empire/

A group of in-liners dedicated to improving New York's skating environment—and having fun while doing it. They publish a newsletter and host a number of night skates (lasting a few hours), day skates (usually half a day), and skating trips (can be two or three days). There are events geared to different skill levels, and their newsletter marks each one clearly. Annual dues are required of members.

Stephen Baum's In-line Skating Clinics & Tours (800-24-SKATE) http://w3.nai.net/~sbaum

Steve organized the city's first skate tour of landmarks and now has three versions: uptown, downtown, and Central Park. Each is a three- to four-hour leisurely skate with a guide and is offered as a private, semiprivate, or group tour. Steve also gives private and group lessons in Central Park, or at any location you choose. To arrange for a private lesson, just call. Note, however, that you can't join a group that's already been formed; you'll have to round up a few friends and assemble one of your own.

Sundance (212-598-4726) PO Box 40314, Brooklyn, NY 11240

A nonprofit corporation that provides the gay and lesbian communities with a range of noncompetitive outdoor activities, including skating. (For more information about Sundance, see page 98.)

Tuesday Night Skate (212-929-0003, ext. 5)

Meets every Tuesday at 8 PM outside Blades West, 72nd Street between Broadway and Columbus Avenue. The size of this group typically varies between 15 and 40, and the skating route varies as well. They sometimes zip down to the South Street Seaport and back, and have also been known to go to Park Slope in Brooklyn, and to a Dairy Queen in Fort Lee, New Jersey. These skates are usually fast-paced and wouldn't be enjoyable for beginners or anyone uncomfortable skating at night in traffic.

Want to Get Aggressive?

Chelsea Piers (212-336-6500) West 23rd Street at the West Side Hwy

The facilities include a skate park with a large half-pipe, a street course—including a fun box and quarter-pipes—and a Vert Ramp. Private lessons are available. Call to find out age and equipment requirements.

Riverside Park

Enter at 108th Street and Riverside Drive and keep heading toward the river. The park is open from noon to 8 PM, Wednesday through Sunday, April 1st to October 30th. There is a $3 admission charge. Full protective gear is required, and anyone under 18 must present a waiver signed by a parent. The park has a 28' wide, 10-1/2' half-pipe (which reaches full vertical), a street course, and about six or seven ramps of various sizes. There are plans to add more goodies.

Aggressively Skating the Net

And if you're *really* into aggressive skating take a look at: http://www.aggroskate.com

The Latest:

In-line figure skating—almost like you see in the Ice Capades—is the latest craze, but you need special in-line pic skates. Each skate has an extension at the front (the pic), which performs the same function as the serrated front edge of ice skate blades. It also has special wheel placement. Given how expensive ice time is, many competitive figure skaters are using these in-line skates for off-ice practice. In any case, with pic skates and some coaching, you can turn, loop, spin, axel, and lutz to your heart's content. If interested, ask at your local skate shop, and look for pic promotions, clinics, and competitions.

Skating the Net

New York City In-line Skating Guide
http://www.skatecity.com/nyc/
Here's all the information you'd ever want on where to skate in Manhattan, Brooklyn, Queens, Staten Island, the Bronx, Westchester, and New Jersey. You will also find the latest on laws and regulations, clubs and organizations, group skates, lessons, teams, and more.

SKATEBOARDING

I GUESS THEY HAD TO DO SOMETHING WHEN THE SURF WASN'T UP, SO SOUTHERN CALIFORNIA SURFERS INVENTED SKATEBOARDING IN THE LATE 50'S BY ATTACHING ROLLER SKATE WHEELS, AXLES, AND SOME PIVOTING HARDWARE TO THE BOTTOM OF PLYWOOD BOARDS. The sport really took off in the mid-70's after the development of faster and more maneuverable polyurethane wheels. Go, dude.

Boarding and Watching

The Astor Cube (at Astor Place and Lafayette Street) is where some of the most happening skateboarders in town can be found. Here are some others: the Museum of Natural History (evenings), the Time-Life Building, The Manhattan side of the Brooklyn Bridge, 6th Avenue between 42nd and 59th Streets, on the banked plazas of the apartment buildings near 95th Street and Columbus Avenue, around the buildings of Battery Park City, and in and around the Wall Street area on weekends. You can also skateboard in the Skate Park in Riverside Park (For more information see page 125.).

13
SPORTS
that get you from
HERE
to
THERE

HIKING

ACCORDING TO SOME STATISTICS, HIKING IS THE MOST POPULAR SPORT IN THE COUNTRY, although I wonder what differentiates an actual hike from having to walk home in the rain when you can't find a cab. Be that as it may, there are numerous forest and mountain trails within five miles of the city, and buses or trains can get you there in 30 to 90 minutes. Departure points include the Port Authority Bus Terminal (8th Avenue and 41st Street), the George Washington Bridge Terminal (Broadway and West 179th Street), Grand Central (Park Avenue and 42nd Street), Penn Station (7th Avenue and 34th Street), the Staten Island Ferry (at South Ferry), or New Jersey Transit in Hoboken, NJ.

Appalachian Mountain Club (212-986-1430)

Sponsors hikes, plus canoeing, fishing trips, and more. (For more information about the club and its activities, see page 101.)

Gateway National Recreation Area

Located at the outer entrance of New York Harbor, this is one of America's first urban national parks. In fact, it's now the sixth most popular national park in the United States, with over seven million visitors per year. Gateway is mile after mile of protected sandy beach, dunes, and wooded parkland. And within it is the **Jamaica Bay Wildlife Refuge** (718-318-4340), where you can see over 300 species of waterfowl. This is a prime migration stop for thousands of water, land, and shore birds. Jamaica Bay has an extensive network of trails, and offers year-round walks, lectures, and events. And all this in Queens!

NY/NJ Trail Conference (212-685-9699) http://www.nynjtc.org/~trails

This all-volunteer organization, founded in 1920 to maintain and build hiking trails in New York and New Jersey, is a great source of information. They will send you a list of outdoor clubs and hiking guides, and tell you how to get to area trails by using public transportation. They also have a lending library and newsletter and sell maps and books.

Outdoor Bound (212-505-1020)

The company arranges hiking trips from one to six days in New York State and throughout the Northeast. The price typically includes equipment rental, lessons, trail fees, transportation, and accommodations when appropriate. Call for a catalog. It contains all their seasonal offerings and includes the degree of difficulty and mileage for each excursion. (For more information about Outdoor Bound see page 101.)

Shore Walkers (212-330-7686)

A nonprofit environmental group interested in preserving the shores and wetlands of New York City and the surrounding area, they host day trips and weekend walking tours. Annual dues get you a quarterly newsletter that lists all their hikes and events, including each one's mileage, pace, and degree of difficulty. The events are free to members, and open to nonmembers for a small guest fee. In addition to their regular activities, Shore Walkers also holds The Great Saunter, an annual 32-mile walk around Manhattan, much of it along the shoreline.

Sierra Club (718-370-2096)

The Sierra Club has a full schedule of year-round hiking and walking events for almost every skill level. (For more information about the Sierra Club, see page 102.)

Sundance (212-598-4726)
PO Box 40314, Brooklyn, NY 11240

Hiking is just one of many activities sponsored by this gay and lesbian-friendly nonprofit corporation. (For more information about Sundance, see page 98.)

Urban Park Rangers (212-427-4040)

Sponsors a full schedule of year-round events, including birding, hawk watches, foliage tours, nature and nocturnal walks, and more. And all this happens in city parks throughout the five boroughs. Call for a free copy of their newsletter.

HORSEBACK RIDING

There is nothing better for the inside of a man than the outside of a horse.

—WINSTON CHURCHILL, English statesman

THE ONLY PEOPLE WHO DON'T BELIEVE Central Park is the greatest park in the world are those who haven't seen it yet or haven't seen enough of it. There are many great ways to experience the park, and one of the best is on a horse.

If you ride well enough, you can have this experience by making arrangements with the Claremont Riding Academy. Although the horse probably knows how to get to the park better than you do, it's a left out of the stable and then a few blocks of clopping along on West 89th Street toward the trees. And this, in fact, is a wonderful hors d'oeuvre. Horses on city streets cause even the most grizzled New Yorkers to smile, and the look of wonderment on faces of children can just about make your day.

Then you arrive at the park and enter an entirely different world. The sounds of the city diminish, your horse's hooves strike dirt instead of concrete. It's quiet enough to hear your saddle creaking and the wind whispering. Since you're atop a horse, you see trees, water, fields, and people from a new height and in a new way, which changes your perspective in more than one way. It slows you down. It lets you breathe. It feels, looks, and sounds different. *Better* different. *Much* better different.

You can make the six-mile northern sweep of the park, which includes the Reservoir and around North Meadow, or you can swing south and ride from the bottom of the reservoir to the playground at the southwest corner of the park, and then back.

On the list of things you should try very hard to do at least once in a lifetime, riding in Central Park falls right between seeing the Grand Canal in Venice, and eating barbecue at Arthur Bryant's in Kansas City.

Riding and Learning

Chelsea Equestrian Center (212-367-9090) West 23rd Street and the Hudson River

This is a high-end, expensive, members-only 30,000 square-foot facility that offers quality and comfort. There is an Olympic-sized indoor ring (180' x 75') with dust-free footing and 24' ceilings, a 150' x 65' outdoor ring, comfortable locker rooms and showers (with private massage rooms and masseurs), full-service tack shop, and a second floor lounge with food and drink that looks onto the indoor ring and out at the river. Chelsea offers a full range of instruction for beginners and up: in hunter/jumper, English, Western, dressage, or simple recreation. The instructors are as good as you'd expect from a facility of this quality; the horses are all carefully chosen and trained in multiple disciplines. Chelsea also offers clinics and seminars and arranges rides in Central Park. If you are serious about riding—or intend to be—and if a stiff price tag won't put you off, this might very well be the place for you.

Claremont Riding Academy (212-724-5100) 175 West 89th Street between Amsterdam and Columbus Avenues

Founded over 100 years ago, this is the oldest continuously operating stable in the country and is housed in what looks like a condemned building. Experienced riders can head for the bridle paths in Central Park, and beginners can get instruction in the stable's small training ring. Both group and private lessons are available. And if you feel like getting out of town, Claremont has the Overpeck Riding Center (201-944-7111), a large facility in New Jersey that you can reach by bus.

Jamaica Bay Riding Academy (718-531-8949) 7000 Shore Parkway, between Broadway Ridge and 70th Street, Brooklyn

Located on some 300 acres along Jamaica Bay, the academy has a 180' x 90' indoor ring, large outdoor jumping and dressage rings, a full tack shop and a restaurant. You can take a guided eight-mile, 45-minute trail ride that wanders along the beach and through the woods or take a private ride with an instructor. Lessons are available from beginning to professional levels. You'll need a car to get here.

Lynne's Riding School (718-261-7679) 88-03 70th Road, Forest Hills

Offers private, semiprivate, and group lessons in half-hour blocks, as well as English or Western trail rides on the bridle paths in nearby Forest Park. Rides are usually scheduled during the day, but you can arrange for one in the evening. The school has an indoor ring and makes every effort to match their instruction to your goals. Lynne's is accessible by subway.

Pelham Bay Stable (718-885-0551)
9 Shore Road, corner of City Island Road, Pelham

This city-owned stable is run by a private company in Pelham Bay Park. Take a one-hour trail ride in the woods and around a golf course or a two-hour jaunt with views of the water during the last hour. You will have a horse that suits your ability level and ride with a guide. The facility has about 25 horses and offers instruction at all levels.

Riverdale Equestrian Centre (718-548-4848)
Broadway and 254th Street

Offers lessons and riding, indoor and out, year-round. They have a 200' x 100' indoor ring, plus outdoor jumping, dressage, and beginner rings. The facility, located on 21 acres in Van Cortlandt Park, used to be a crumbling city-run affair until two ex-Olympians took it over and turned it into a first-rate operation. It's a subway ride and 12-block walk to get there.

Sundance (212-598-4726)
PO Box 40314, Brooklyn, NY 11240

A nonprofit corporation that provides the gay and lesbian communities with a range of noncompetitive outdoor activities, including Western and English riding. (For more information about Sundance, see page 98.)

RACEWALKING

SOMETIMES YOU HAVE TO SUFFER FOR YOUR ART, and racewalking is no exception. To the uninitiated observer, race walkers look funny. It's not the awkwardness of a beginner that's the problem, it's the racewalking itself. It's the piston-pumping arms, the exaggerated hip-swinging, the heel/toe, heel/toe, heel-toe gait—and the scrunched-up, determined look that all race walkers seem to have. Looks aside, racewalking is a terrific cardiovascular workout. It's a great way to meet people. It gets you out in the fresh air, is much easier of the knees than running, and not very hard to learn. Plus you can racewalk until you're very old.

Walking and Learning

Front Runners (212-724-9700)

Founded in 1979 to promote racewalking (as well as running, track, cycling) in the gay and lesbian communities, Front Runners offers classes, noncompetitive racewalks in various parts of the metropolitan area, and a wide range of social events and activities.

Park Racewalkers (212-628-1317)
320 East 83rd Street, Box 18, 2New York, NY 10028

The club has distance and speed workouts four or five times during the week in Central Park, as well as weekend workouts (followed by brunch at a nearby restaurant). Beginner sessions are offered on weekends all the time, and on weekdays by appointment only. The club, which was founded in 1989 to enourage participation in the sport, sponsors nine races each year and encourages members who aren't racing to help out with the events. There are annual dues, which get you a T-shirt, mailings about club activities, and a newsletter. The club also sponsors a variety of social events.

New York Road Runners Club (212-423-2292) http://www.nyrrc.org/

The world's largest running club, with over 30,000 members, also offers racewalking classes on weekday evenings from April to September in Central Park. (For more information about the New York Road Runners Club see page 134.)

New York Walkers Club (Jake Jacobson at 516-731-5255)

The club promotes "health" walking, which is a modified racewalking exercise. Members work out and receive free instruction in Central Park 50 weeks a year. If you want to compete, you can join the *East Side Racewalk Team.* For more information send a SASE to Jake Jacobson, 33 Saddle Lane, Levittown, NY, 11756. Jake has Olympic and National Team coaching experience, and is one of the most experienced racewalking coaches in the country.

Riverbank State Park (212-694-3600) On the Hudson River at 145th Street

Three days a week, a club for early-bird race walkers club meets on the eight-lane, four laps/mile track that circles the football/soccer /baseball field. The track is open from the beginning of March through the end of October and can be used for working out unless a scheduled event is taking place.

RUNNING

The only reason I would take up jogging is so that I could hear heavy breathing again. —IRMA BOMBECK, author and humorist

Running Out and About

People run everywhere in this town, and some of the most popular spots include Central Park's outer loop (six miles), cut-off loop (which is four miles and crosses the 102nd Street service road), lower loop (one mile) and Reservoir (85th to 96th Street). The Reservoir, in fact, is probably the single most popular running spot in town. It is a 1.58 mile loop that's enhanced by fabulous city views and punctuated with "Hey! Wasn't that?" celebrity alerts. Reservoir etiquette dictates a counter-clockwise jog, so if you keep bumping into people, you're probably running the wrong way. Popular running routes outside of Central Park include: Riverside Park along the Hudson (72nd to 116th Street and back is four and one-half miles), Washington Square Park (where you run around the outside of Waverly Place, University Place, West 4th, and MacDougal), along the East River from the 60's up to 96th Street, and the Battery Park Esplanade (about two miles).

Tracks: Outdoors and Indoors

Asphalt Green (212-369-8890)
555 East 90th Street at York Avenue

An outdoor track (four laps/mile) circles the beautiful, artificial turf football/soccer/baseball field, and a short indoor track (26 laps/mile and pretty claustrophobic) circles the top of the main gym. The outdoor track is open to anyone as long as it's not being used for an organized event. Membership at Asphalt Green is required if you want to use the indoor track.

Carmine Recreation Center (212-242-5228)
Clarkson Street & 7th Avenue South

The padded indoor 32 laps/mile track is even shorter and more claustrophobic than the one at Asphalt Green. It circles the top of their two gyms.

Central Park
At around 86th Street

There is an eight laps/mile track near the Metropolitan Museum of Art. It circles the basketball and volleyball courts.

Chelsea Piers (212-336-6000)
West 23rd Street at the West Side Hwy

Chelsea has a four-lane, four laps/mile indoor running track, plus a six-lane, 200 meter banked, competition track. This is a beautiful track that makes for very good people watching.

McBurney YMCA (212-741-9210)
215 West 23rd Street between 7th and 8th Avenues

Offers a 20 laps/mile banked, indoor track.

Reebok (212-362-6800)
160 Columbus Avenue between 67th and 68th Street

The three-lane, six laps/mile track circles the outside of the building six floors up. The interesting city views make running here quite pleasurable, especially on a clear sunny day.

Riverbank State Park (212-694-3600)
On the Hudson River at 145th Street

An eight-lane, four laps/mile track that circles the football/soccer/baseball field is open from the beginning of March through the end of October. Three days per week, Riverbank has an early-bird runners club. The track can be used by the public for workouts as long as a scheduled event is not taking place.

Riverside Park
Near 74th Street
Has an eight laps/mile outdoor track.

YWCA (212-755-2700)
610 Lexington Avenue at 53rd Street
The facility has a padded, indoor 26 laps/mile track.

Running Clubs

Achilles (212-354-0300)

Offers training and coaching to runners and racers with disabilities.

Central Park Track Club (212-838-1120)

Founded in 1972, this club now boasts about 300 members who participate in everything from recreational running, sprints, and relays to marathons (the club usually fields one of the largest teams in the NYC Marathon) and even ultramarathons. Organized workouts are held throughout the year in Central Park and at the track in East River Park. The workouts move indoors during the winter. Membership in the club includes coaching, club parties and functions, participation in team events, and a newsletter. There is no pressure in this club to perform at any particular level, or to run in any number of races. Instead, there's *encouragement* to race because it's good motivation to maintain a high fitness level. Club members range in age from 20 to 70, and about 25% are women. To learn more about the club, just show up at one of the workouts. except on major holidays, or when lousy whether intervenes. These are held Thursday evenings at 7 PM (in Central Park, by the statue of Daniel Webster at the intersection of West Drive and West 72nd Street), or Tuesdays at 7 PM from April through October at the East River Park Track oval (6th Street and the FDR Drive). Workouts are not held on major holidays or in bad weather.

Front Runners (212-724-9700)

Founded in 1979 to promote running in the gay and lesbian communities—as well as racewalking, track, and cycling. Front Runners offers classes and noncompetitive fun runs from one to six miles in various parts of the metropolitan area. They also sponsor a wide range of social activities.

Moving Comfort (212-222-7216 or 212-628-8823)

This women's distance racing team (1,500 meters and up) has been sponsored by the Moving Comfort clothing company since 1992. They compete at a very high level, so only serious runners need apply. The members of Moving Comfort work out twice a week, and participate in numerous competitions.

New York Flyers Running Club (212-466-9786)

The club includes runners at all ability levels, including those interested in biathlons and triathlons. About 70% of the members live in Manhattan, and the age breakdown is: 25% in their twenties, 50% in their thirties, and 25% forty-plus. The ten-year-old club offers group workouts three times a week, and clinics on running form, stretching, and other topics. There is coaching, customized training programs, and speed classes one night a week, plus a full range of social and charitable events (including dinners, parties, and brunches). Your annual dues entitle you to a monthly newsletter, and access to the club's telephone hotline and e-mail network.

New York Road Runners Club (212-423-2292) http://www.nyrrc.org/

The world's largest running club, with over 30,000 members, the NYRRC hosts over 1,200 running events every year. No matter what your interest or skill level, there will likely be a class or event for you. The club has daily runs, weekly races, and is probably best known as the sponsor of the New York City Marathon and the New Year's Eve Midnight Run. The website lists race results, race and event schedules, training tips, membership information, and a full list of classes—including *seven* different levels of running, yoga, deep water running, and racewalking.

The New York City Marathon is run on the first Sunday in November, covers 26.2 miles through all five boroughs, and typically attracts almost 30,000 runners. Here are some notable facts about the race: The night before the event, runners consume 9,000 pounds of pasta. At the start of the race, they slog through 14,000 cups of yogurt and wake up with 75,000 cups of coffee. During the race, they rehydrate with 22,000 gallons of Gatorade and 184,000 bottles of spring water.

The New Year's Eve Midnight Run is an annual 5K race that starts and ends at Tavern on the Green (67th Street and West Drive). People run in costumes and drink champagne. It's terrific fun and a *real* New York experience. Contact the NYRRC if you want to join the race, or just show up to watch.

Warren Street (212-807-7422)

A club for competitive running and (non-competitive) socializing. The club enters teams and individuals in various area races, and although running instruction is available and runners at all levels are welcome, if you're a beginner, you'll probably start off as more of a social member.

Classes

Super Runners Shop (212-787-7665)
77th Street and Columbus Avenue

Weekly classes and clinics are hosted by Mike Keohane, an experienced track coach, Olympics Trials qualifier, and veteran of 12 marathons. Novice and intermediate runners are welcome on Mondays, more advanced runners on Tuesdays, and Mike has clinics with guest speakers on Thursdays. The classes are offered in ten-session packages, and class size is limited. Call the store for current schedules, information, and costs.

Did you know?

That the first Boston Marathon (April 19, 1897) was won by John J. McDermott, who represented the Pastime Athletic Club and covered the course in 2:55:10? He was—*what else*—a New Yorker.

That Brooklyn's own Bishop Loughlin High School Band has performed at the last 17 marathons, and played the theme from *Rocky* an average of 300 times each?

SKIING AND SNOWBOARDING

The sport of skiing consists of wearing three thousand dollars' worth of clothes and equipment and driving two hundred miles in the snow in order to stand at a bar and get drunk. —P.J. O'ROURKE, humorist

WITH ENOUGH SNOW ON THE GROUND, you can have a great time cross-country skiing almost anywhere in the five boroughs—but for downhill, you really have to get out of town.

Blades West (212-787-3911)
120 West 72nd Street between Columbus Avenue and Broadway
Takes mostly snowboarders about 1-1/2 hours to New York State's Hunter Mountain. You can arrange a trip with or without rentals, and they throw in a free lesson.

Island Tours (718-343-4444)
Leaves for Windham (in New York State, about 2-1/2 hours away) from the Grand Hyatt, on 42nd Street near Lexington Avenue, three times during the week and on Sunday. The fee includes lift tickets, a VCR-equipped bus, and refreshments.

Miramar Ski Club (212-978-9191)
A private, nonprofit organization that owns a lodge in Waitsfield, Vermont and runs weekly bus trips there. Every year they also sponsor a week-long ski trip—either out West or to Europe—as well as many off-season activities.

Paragon Sporting Goods
(212-255-8036, ext. 256)
18th Street and Broadway
Runs ski and snowboard trips to Hunter Mountain twice a week starting in January. Bring your own equipment or rent. The trip cost cost includes round-trip bus fare, lift tickets, and breakfast. Lessons are available.

Peak Experience (212-982-5007)
http://www.peaks.com
Arranges ski trips to New Hampshire (Attitash Bear Peak), Vermont (Haystack, Killington, Mount Snow, Sugarbush, Pico), and Maine (Sugarloaf and Sunday River). They offer special deals and packages. The website gives you snow reports, as well as resort facts, figures, and photos (the images are updated daily).

Sierra Club (718-370-2096)
The Sierra Club has an extensive schedule of ski trips for almost every interest and skill level. (For more information about the Sierra Club, see page 102.)

Snow Flyers (212-439-4799)
http://www.snowflyers.com/snowflyers.htm
The club organizes trips to Northeastern resorts and to two major western destinations each year.

The goal is to ski and board, economically, in as many places as possible. Established in 1996 by skiers and snowboarders in the tri-state area, the club's members range in age from 22 to 45, and are mostly single and social.

Sundance
(212-598-4726)
PO Box 40314, Brooklyn, NY 11240
Provides the gay and lesbian communities with a range of noncompetitive outdoor activities, including downhill and cross-country skiing. (For more information about Sundance, see page 98.)

Cross-Country Skiing

Outdoor Bound (212-505-1020)
Arranges day trips (about an hour's drive from town) and overnight cross-country ski trips to various destinations in New York State and throughout the Northeast. You can even try snowshoeing with them. Equipment rental, lessons, trail fees, guides for beginners, and transportation are included in the price. (For more information about Outdoor Bound, see page 102.)

Skiing the Net

http://www.nynow.com/nysol/skiing.html
Find New York Sports Online links to over 30 skiing areas and destinations countrywide, from New York and the rest of the Northeast to Colorado, New Mexico, Montana, and Wyoming. This is a good place to start if you're just beginning to look around for skiing options.

Skiing and Snowboarding Simulator

The New York Health & Racquet Club
(212-422-4653)
39 Whitehall Street, between Pearl and Water Streets
This club's virtual reality ski and snowboard simulator, a huge treadmill-like affair, gives you a great workout opportunity. You're strapped into a harness and an instructor matches the speed and tilt of the machine to your individual skill level. While skiing or boarding, you view images on a large video screen which make you feel as though you're cascading down the slopes at Vail. The simulator is available to members and non-members and is effective as a learning tool. The hourly rate includes a lesson and equipment.

INDEX

LET'S HEAR FROM YOU

PLEASE WRITE ME WITH YOUR COMMENTS ABOUT THE LISTINGS IN *SPORTS NEW YORK*. What are *your* experiences with the facilities, clubs, teams, organizations, and companies in the book? Where do you do what you do? And why do you think other people should know about it? And also, let me know about listings you'd like to see included in the next edition.

Steve Schwartz
Sports New York
c/o City and Company
22 West 23rd Street
New York, NY 10010

ABOUT THE AUTHOR

STEVE'S MEDICAL HISTORY INCLUDES broken fingers from baseball, a bad knee from volleyball, pulled back muscles from whitewater rafting, a broken nose from basketball, a strained wrist from tennis, a fractured arm from football, a twisted ankle from racquetball, a pulled hamstring from running, and a hyper-extended elbow from squash. Then there's the hook he embedded in his hand while learning to fish. Steve is *not* a klutz. It's just that if you play sports long enough . . . stuff happens.

Steve Schwartz lives in Manhattan with his workout-enthusiast wife and volleyball-playing daughter. If you see him on some field or in a schoolyard, or a gym, he's the 6'4", 230-lb., bearded, 50ish, stylish left-hander who looks like he's lost a step or two but can still kick a little ass. Say hello. Could be him.

NEW YORK COOL & CLASSIC

Would you like to receive City & Company's **25 Cool and Classic Places to Go in New York?** It's free. Just share with us your favorite New York spot. If you like. If not, simply fill in this form and mail, fax, or e-mail it to us. So the next time someone says, "What do you want to do this weekend?," maybe you'll surprise them!

NAME ______________________________

ADDRESS ______________________________

____

RETURN TO: City & Company
22 West 23rd Street New York, New York 10010
Fax 212.242.0500
E-mail Cityco @ bway.net

ACKNOWLEDGMENTS

I'D LIKE TO THANK HELENE SILVER FOR HER VISION OF AN ENTIRE COMPANY DEDICATED TO PUBLISHING TERRIFIC BOOKS ABOUT THE GREATEST CITY IN THE WORLD, AND TIM HAFT FOR HIS INVALUABLE CONTRIBUTIONS TO THE MANUSCRIPT. Thanks go to my family as well: to Sarah Jane Freymann, my wife and agent, for her ongoing forbearance as each sports season inexorably slides into the next—day after day, week after week, month after month, and year after year; to my daughter Elisabeth for the great pleasure she gave me watching her tremendous growth as a high school varsity volleyball player, and to my brother, Ken—even though he realized my mother's worst nightmare by breaking my nose one day in a basketball game. I'm also grateful for the sports genes inherited from my grandfather, a minor league pitcher in the New York Giants farm system, and my father, a DeWitt Clinton High School football player.

Finally, I'd like to thank the 1973 champion New York Knicks who were responsible for the absolutely best sports season of my life. And yes, I was actually sitting in the Garden when Willis Reed dragged his bad leg onto the court, hit his first two jump shots over Wilt Chamberlain, and helped propel this team into the highest reaches of sports legend.

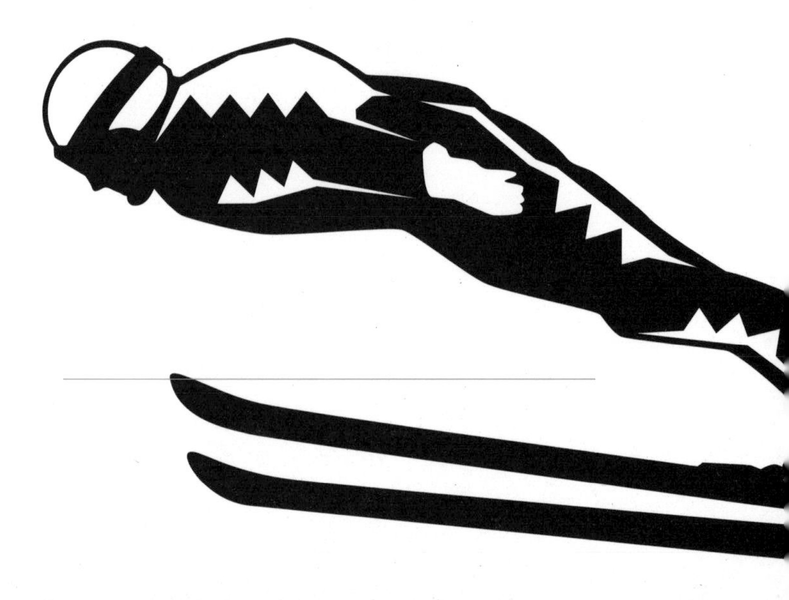